HISTORY of WOMEN'S COSTUME

MARION SICHEL

Batsford Academic and Educational Ltd   *London*

First published 1984
Reprinted 1985

Typeset by Tek-Art Ltd, Kent
and printed in Great Britain by
The Anchor Press Ltd
Tiptree, Essex
for the publishers
Batsford Academic and Educational Ltd
an imprint of B T Batsford Ltd
4 Fitzhardinge Street
London W1H 0AH

British Library Cataloguing in Publication Data

Sichel, Marion
    History of women' costume—(Costume reference)
    1. Costume—History
    I. Title   II. Series
    391'.2'09   GT1720

ISBN 0 7134 1515 0

Index

contrasting colour.

Plumpers Small cork balls put into the mouth to fill out hollow cheeks.

Points Ties with decorated metal tips.

Polonaise Boned bodice cut away to reveal a waistcoat, and the skirt in three drapes with drawstrings, revealing the petticoat beneath.

Princes style Bodice and skirt in one without a waist seam, the skirts being gored.

Pumps Soft, flat heeled shoes with thin soles.

Rebato Starched or wire support for large ruffs around a low necked bodice.

Reefer Long jacket or thigh length coat.

Reticule Small handbag.

Revers Turned-back edge of a coat, waistcoat or jacket.

Robe a l'Anglaise Sac-back gown with the pleats sewn to waist level.

Robings Flat trimmings or borders.

Round gown Bodice and skirt in one, and closed.

Ruff Circular collar, starched and gathered at neck or wrist.

Sac back Box pleats sewn from neck to shoulder, then allowed to hang loose behind.

Slashings Slits cut into garments in symetrical designs to allow the lining or undergarment to be pulled through.

Spencer Short waist length jacket.

Steinkirk Long lace edged cravat knotted beneath the chin.

Stola Loose overgarment, sometimes worn with two belts.

Stomacher Inverted triangular front part covering a low décolletage.

Sugarloaf hat High conical crown and a broad rolled brim.

Surcote or **Supertunic** Garment worn over a tunic.

Taffeta pipkin Flat crowned hat, pleated to a narrow brim.

Tailor-made Two-piece costume, made by a tailor rather than a dressmaker.

Teagown Informal afternoonwear.

Templers Ornamental metal bosses enclosing hair either side of the face supported by a connecting fillet or headdress.

Tippet Short shoulder cape.

Toque Brimless hat, made similar to a turban.

Tour False curls added to the front hair.

Tucker Frilled edging to a low necked bodice.

Turban Material placed in folds around the head.

Ulster Overcoat with a whole or half belt.

Welt Strengthened edge of a garment.

Whisk Broad lace trimmed falling collar, similar to a gorget.

Wimple Piece of material draped under the chin and pinned to the hair either side.

Wings Decorative stiffened crescent shaped bands extending over the shoulder seams.

Zone Fill-in for an open bodice.

Bibliography

Amphlett, Hilda, *Hats*, Sadler 1974

Arnold, J, *Handbook of Costume*, Macmillan 1973

Arnold, J, *Patterns of Fashion* 2 vols, Macmillan 1972

Asser, Joyce, *Historic Hairdressing*, Pitman 1966

Barfoot, A, *Everyday Costume in England*, Batsford 1961

Boehn, Max van, *Modes and Manners* (8 vols), Harrap 1926

Bott, Alan, *Our Mothers*, Gollanz 1932

Boucher, F, *20,000 Years of Fashion*, Abrams; *History of Costume in the West*, Thames and Hudson 1967

Bradfield, N, *Historical Costumes of England* Harrup 1958

Brooke, Iris, *History of English Costume*, Methuen 1937

Buck, Anne, *Victorian Costume & Costume Accessories*, Jenkins 1961

Calthrop, D C, *English Costume*, A and C Black 1906

Carter, Ernestine, *Twentieth Century Fashion*, Eyre Methuen 1975

Cassin-Scott, J, *Costume and Fashion 1550-1760*, Blandford 1975

Cassin-Scott, J, *Costume and Fashion 1760-1920*, Blandford 1971

Clinch, George, *English Costume*, E P Publishing 1975

Contini, M, *Fashion from Ancient Egypt to the Present Day*, Hamlyn 1967

Cooke, P C, *English Costume*, Gallery Press 1968

Corson, R, *Fashions in Make-up*, Peter Owen 1972

Courtais, C De, *Women's Headdress and Hairstyles in England*, Batsford 1975

Cunnington, C W and P, *Handbook of English Costume* (6 vols), Faber 1969-1975

Cunnington-Beard, *Dictionary of English Costume*, A and C Black 1972

Davenport, M, *The Book of Costume*, Bonanza 1968

Dorner, Jane, *Fashion*, Octopus 1974

Ewing, E, *Fashion in Underwear*, Batsford 1971

Fairholt, F W, *Costume in England*, Bell 1885

Garland, M, *The Changing Face of Beauty*, Weidenfeld and Nicholson 1957; *History of Fashion*, Orbis 1975

Gernsheim, Alison, *Fashion and Reality* Faber 1963

Gibbs-Smith, Charles, *The Fashionable Lady in the Nineteenth Century*, HMSO 1960

Gorsline, D, *What People Wore*, Bonanza 1951

Gunn, Fenja, *The Artificial Face*, David and Charles 1973

Halls, Z, *Women's Costumes 1750-1800*, HMSO 1972

Hansen, H, *Costume Cavalcade*, Methuen 1956

Harrison, Molly, *Hairstyles and Hairdressing*, Ward Lock 1968

Hill, M H and Bucknell, P A, *The Evolution of Fashion*, Batsford 1967

Hill, G, *History of English Dress* (2 vols), Bentley 1893

Holland, V, *Hand Coloured Fashion Plates 1770-1899*, Batsford 1955

Koehler, C, *History of Costume*, Constable 1963

Laver, James, *Concise History of Costume*, Thames and Hudson 1963; *Costume*, Batsford 1956; *Costume through the Ages*, Thames and Hudson 1964; *Fashion and Fashion Plates 1800-1900*, King Penguin 1943

Lister, Margot, *Costume*, Jenkins 1967

Monsarrat, A, *And the Bride Wore . . .*, Gentry Books 1973

Moore, D, *Fashion Through Fashion Plates 1771-1870*, Ward Lock 1971

Norris, Herbert, *Costume & Fashion*, Dent 1924

Pistolese and Horstig, *History of Fashions*, Wiley 1970

Planche, J R, *British Costume*, C Cox 1847

Saint-Laurent, C, *History of Ladies Underwear*, Joseph 1968

Strutt, J, *Complete View of the Dress Habits of the People of England* (2 vols), H C Bohn 1842

Truman, N, *Historic Costuming*, Pitman 1956

Waugh, Norah, *The Cut of Women's Clothes 1600-1930 Faber 1968; Corsets and Crinolines*, Batsford 1970

Wilcox, R T, *Dictionary of Costume*, Batsford 1970; *The Mode in Costume*, Scribner 1942; *The Mode in Hats and Headdress*, Scribner 1948

Wilson, E, *History of Shoe Fashions*, Pitman 1969

Yarwood, D, *Encyclopaedia of World Costume*, Batsford 1967

Yarwood, D, *English Costume from the 2nd Century BC to the Present Day*, Batsford 1975

Yarwood, D, *Outline on English Costume*, Batsford 1967

Yarwood, D, *Lady's Realm*, Arrow Books 1972

Yarwood, D, *Pictorial Encyclopaedia of Fashion*, Hamlyn 1968

Yarwood, D, *Victorian Fashions from Harpers Bazaar 1867-1898*, Dover 1974

Contents

The full skirt of the travelling costume was concealed by a large cloak, *c* 1880

Both day dresses had wide puffed sleeves giving a broader appearance.
The girl on the left has demi gigot sleeves with ornate mancherons. The full
skirts extended with petticoats are ankle length. The dainty shoes are tied
with cross ribboning, like ballet shoes, *c* 1830

Caption to illustration on title page
The partlet is finished with a small high neck ruff. The overskirt is open in an
inverted V in the front, being folded back and held in place with ribbon loops.
The back view shows the wide turned-back sleeves and the English version
of the Spanish farthingale worn beneath a trained skirt. It also shows the
back of the French hood with the flat tube hanging down, *c* 1560

Introduction

In writing a book of costume reference it is extremely difficult to decide what to include and what to omit, but hopefully this book may nevertheless prove a useful source of reference.

Fashion establishes its own equilibrium and when something is taken away from one section of dress, something else appears in another to balance the loss. For instance, the introduction of masks in the sixteenth century coincided with the fashion for low cut bodices.

Fashionable dress has seldom been designed for comfort. The main influences on designers have customarily been the demands of style and coquetry. Ease of wear has usually been ignored. The idea of dressing suitably for particular seasons and occasions is comparatively new.

Architectural styles are invariably echoed in the fashions of the day. In the 1870s and 1880s, for instance, houses were built with greenhouses attached to the back, giving the effect of bustles. In the early twentieth century blouses resembled the overhanging balconies on houses.

With the rising of the feminist movement women copied the prevailing male fashion for straw boaters and cloth caps; even the high stiff-collared blouses were similar to men's shirts and were often worn with ties – at least until the First World War.

The sixteenth century was the true age of the fashion doll. European travel became freer and what began as an aristocratic whim developed into an important part of the high fashion trade of the seventeenth century. Dolls, called *Pandoras*, were first sent out by French fashion houses, not only for details of dress, but also for their *coiffures*.

Fashion dolls had already existed as early as the fourteenth century, when an English Queen had the latest French styles sent over from Paris, thus confirming the early pre-eminence of the French capital in the realm of fashion. Then, as later, dolls were the most efficient means of conveying in detail the prevailing modes. As their importance grew, Pandoras became known as *Poupées de la Rue St-Honoré*. although these fashion dolls started by being slightly larger than dolls as playthings, they eventually became life-size so that the ladies could actually try on the garments, just as model dresses are bought today.

It is not the famous fashion houses or the designers who set the fashions; they just interpret the prevailing moods which are then made fashionable by the women who follow the modes and are seen to wear designer clothes. What looks beautiful now will look hideous presently, for concepts of beauty and ugliness are constantly changing.

The Fashion Cycle

A dress seems immodest ten years before its time
Shameless five years before its time
Daring one year before its time, then fashionable
Unfashionable one year after its time
Hideous ten years after its time
Ridiculous twenty years after its time
Curious thirty years after its time
Amusing fifty years after its time
Enchanting seventy years after its time
Romantic one hundred years after its time
Exceedingly beautiful one hundred and fifty years after its time.

Grecian headdresses and headwear

Ancient Greek dress

The pelpos falls in pleats to the ankles and is held in place by a girdle around the waist, and fibulae at the shoulders. A kerchief covers the head

Greek costume depended for its style on drapery as can be seen portrayed in contemporary sculptures. First the Dorians and later the Ionians influenced the styles. A long *chiton* was generally worn beneath a *peplos* by the Dorian women and over this a *chlamys* which was in Doric times a gaily patterned woollen cloak. In the Ionic period it was made of soft linen. The peplos was worn as an outer garment. Basically it was a wide piece of material forming a kind of shawl which was fastened at the shoulder and open on one side, falling in folds, with a richly patterned border around the edges. When long, it was pouched over a belt to fall loosely.

Hairstyles

Hair was generally worn long with a centre parting, braided and drawn into a knot at the back. It was often tinted – blond being the most popular colour. Elaborately carved combs and circlets held the hair in place.

Wigs too were fashionable, dressed in diverse styles, and adorned with wreaths or coronets of flowers or jewellery. Although seldom worn, hats were bulbous with a pointed top and wide brim, known as a *tholia*. A kerchief was the more usual form of head covering.

Footwear

As most women spent a great deal of time in the home, they usually wore open sandals, the soles attached with straps which fastened in various ways, mainly passing between the toes.

Accessories and make-up

Bracelets, often of precious metals, were worn round the wrists as well as on the upper arms and ankles. *Necklaces, pendants*, and *amulets*, worn to ward off evil spirits, were usually made of gold. *Earrings* were also fashionable, the ears being pierced.

Greek women made great use of make-up, using beauty creams, rouge and perfumes. Eye make-up was also used on a large scale in order to make the eyes look larger.

Chiton worn with a himation as an outdoor garment that wrapped around the shoulders and could partially hide the face

Ancient Roman dress

Overtunic worn with stola

Typical Roman footwear

Both men and women wore similar garments. Their basic garment, a *stola*, was similar to the Ionic chiton, and corresponded to the male tunic and toga. It was held on the hips and below the breast with girdles, or was allowed to hang down to the ground. It was fuller than the sleeveless tunic over which it was worn. A breast band, or *strophium*, was worn next to the skin, and was in fact one of the earliest forms of brassière. Over the *stola* a voluminous cloak known as a *palla*, similar to the Greek peplos was also worn. This was fastened on the left shoulder with a *fibula*.

Headwear and hairstyles

During the Roman Republic hairstyles were simple, with just rows of curls across the forehead and a knot at the nape of the neck enclosed with a *caul*, often richly adorned with precious stones. Greek fashions were also copied using the *chignon*. As the Romans became wealthier, hairstyles became more ornate. Curls, locks, plaits and waves were arranged with hot curling irons in such complicated styles that special hairdressers often had to be employed. If their own hair was insufficient, false hair was added to give extra height. These hairstyles were profusely decorated with gold, pearls and other precious stones, as well as with garlands and ribbons which were entwined in the hair.

In public, women covered their heads with veils or the folds of the *palla*.

Footwear

Sandals were worn indoors. The *calceus*, worn out of doors, consisted of leather soles with thonging crossing over the feet and up part of the legs. They could be richly embellished with fringes and gold embroidery as well as precious stones.

Socks, made of wool, were worn in cooler weather.

Accessories

The luxury in jewellery corresponded with the general wealth of the people. *Rings, bracelets, earrings, pendants* and *anklets* were made of gold and precious stones.

Beauty accessories such as face patches, powder, rouge, eyeblack, as well as a great selection of perfumes and hair oils, were used in

Roman dress as depicted on a statue. The sleeveless undertunic is partially covered by the stola. The overall appearance is similar to a male toga

abundance. Roman women used lead oxide, chalk and coloured paints on their faces, and even wore false teeth made of wax.

Fans and *umbrellas* were carried. *Belts* were worn with purses attached for carrying valuables.

The stiff curls are supported on a frame in front, whilst the back hair is coiled in a bun

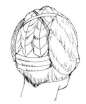

The hair is plaited close to the head

Roman headwear and hairstyles

Ancient and Roman Britain

The hair, often long and plaited, is hidden beneath a fine linen veil hanging loosely behind and held in place with a narrow band or circlet

Women's clothing altered little during the Roman influence. They wore two tunics, the overtunic being shorter with loose sleeves. This tunic reached the thighs, whilst the other went down to the ankles.

Various kinds of cloth were manufactured in Gaul made of fine wool, often woven in checks or stripes. Long flowing gowns, often sleeveless, had a belt at the waist. Short sleeved gowns were worn beneath short sleeved overtunics. Occasionally skirts and tops were separate, leaving a bare midriff, the skirts being held up with either braces or a drawstring.

Headwear and hairstyles
Celtic women had shoulder length hair, sometimes plaited. Headwear consisted of the cloak or cape being pulled over the head.

Accessories
Jewellery consisted or *rings, bracelets, necklaces* made of twisted gold or silver wire, of Celtic or Roman styles. *Pins* and *brooches* were also popular.

Footwear
A piece of leather pulled around the foot and laced with thongs, formed a single shoe. *Sandals*, similar to those worn by the Ancient Greeks and Romans, were also seen.

Roman influence. Over the long stola is worn a short tunic held in at the waist with a belt. The head is covered with a palla

Leather pulled up around the foot and laced with thonging to form a shoe

Saxons and Normans

Costumes in the post Roman period changed little. A close fitting ground length *kirtle* or tunic, worn over a chemise shirt, was put on over the head. The long tight sleeves often had cuffs. Over the kirtle was worn a supertunic or *roc*. This, like the kirtle was put on over the head but was fuller, falling to the ground, and often hitched up with a girdle revealing the kirtle beneath. The supertunic was usually embroidered around the neck, cuffs and hem. As Englishwomen were renowned for their needlework, this was invariably very lavish. In Norman times the sleeves of the supertunic were often long and bell shaped, coming well over the hands, so that they could be used as muffs.

Mantles were usually cut square and reached the ground. They were closed all round and put on over the head. Sometimes they were lined in a contrasting colour and hitched up in the front. Unlike those of the men they did not have any attached hoods.

A ground length kirtle with long tight fitting sleeves is worn beneath the supertunic with a waist girdle. This is embroidered around the cuffs, hem and neck. The neck is hidden by a veil that covers the hair and is draped around the neck and shoulders, c 1130

Mantle worn over a kirtle that had hem and cuffs embroidered. The hair is covered by a headraile draped around the neck, the ends hanging behind. Anglo-Saxon period

Footwear
Heelless shoes and sandals, similar to the men's, were mainly of leather and low cut, held on with thonging.

Cloth stockings were cut on the cross to give a better fit. They were fastened by ties.

Headwear and hairstyles
Veils or *headrailes*, as they were called by the Saxons, were worn indoors as well as outdoors. They covered the head from the forehead and were draped down the back, completely covering the hair. These headrailes, rather like stoles with the ends draped in various ways, were in matching or contrasting colours to the supertunic. Although the hair was concealed it was often plaited with gold hairpins that held both the hair and veil in place. Only single girls were permitted to wear their hair loose and uncovered during the Anglo-Saxon period. During the Norman period the headrailes became smaller and were known as *couvrechief*. They were rectangular or round. The straight edge lay across the forehead covering the hair, and the bulk of the material was then allowed to hang in folds to the shoulders, the ends arranged like a scarf.

Accessories
Jewellery was very fashionable and represented in gold and jewelled *circlets, neckbands, bracelets, rings* and *hairpins*.

11

Mediaeval

twelfth to fifteenth century

The gown is high waisted with the skirt falling in heavy folds to the ground. The neckline and cuffs of the long sleeves and the hem of the skirt are all fur trimmed. The eyebrows and forehead hair is plucked and the truncated headdresss has a butterfly-shaped veil, c 1484

The long low-necked gown fastened at the back with lacing to just below the waist. The skirt hangs in heavy folds to the ground. The long cuffs are knotted to prevent them trailing to the ground. The long hair parted in the centre is plaited, and a circlet is also worn

Only a very gradual change began to take place at the start of the twelfth century, and this was mainly only for the wealthier ladies.

Kirtles, which had remained unchanged until about 1330, became more shaped to the figure, with the skirt in full folds falling to the ground. The low neckline often revealed the shoulders. Bodices were made to fit closer to hip level with the skirt often trained and fuller than previously. Fastening was with laces, front or back, as these styles were too tight to go over the head as previously. Sleeves were generally close fitting to the elbows and then became bell shaped. When very long, they sometimes had the cuffs to ground level, and these were tied in knots. Girdles were worn around the hips with the ends hanging down, almost to the ground.

Towards the end of the fifteenth century kirtles were gradually replaced by the *houppelande*. In the early part of the fifteenth century the houppelande had a high-necked collar and was put on over the head. The neckline could be V shaped. This opening became broad and revealed the garment beneath, either kirtle or *cote-hardie*. The sleeves, usually tubular (the bagpipe shape only being popular between about 1400-1430) were the most fashionable. By the 1470s the bodice was closer fitting to hip level, and the skirt often trained. The neckline was usually low and filled in with a gorget or neckerchief. Edges could be fur trimmed.

A gown, known as a *surcote* in the thirteenth century, did not alter a great deal. The main innovation was that the neckline became lower with a V shaped opening. The fullness was retained, and about the middle of the twelfth century pockets or *fitchets* were included. Through these placket holes, items, such as purses or pomandas suspended from the girdle around the chemise, could be reached. Sleeveless surcotes were also worn. These had just slits for the arms to protrude, and like the sleeved version were worn loose without a girdle. They were often fur lined for the winter.

Surcotes remained popular throughout the fourteenth century. In the middle of the century the sleeveless version developed into a sideless style, open from the shoulders to the hips, revealing the undergarment with girdle. This was called a *tabard*. The front panel, giving a *stomacher* effect, was often decorated and trimmed with fur.

The *cote-hardie* was generally low necked and fastened down to the waist. The elbow length sleeves had long hanging cuffs, known as *tippets*. By the end of the fourteenth century it became fastened down to the hem. Placket slits or fitchets in the skirts were popular. After the 1450s the cote-

The fur-trimmed surcote has long, tight sleeves and the long skirt is gathered at the hips, c 1380

hardie was being replaced by the houppelande, then known as a *gown*. It was a large overgarment falling in tubular folds, the length varying from thigh to ground. The gown was close fitting at the bodice with the skirt in folds. Girdles were worn at the hips. The sleeves were buttoned from the elbows to the wrists and widened over the hands to the knuckles or covering the second finger joint.

Outdoor wear

Cloaks did not alter greatly, although attached hoods (many fur lined) for warmth when travelling became popular and remained fashionable until about 1450. Long protrusions to the hoods called *liripipes* were often seen. The cloaks were generally ground length and sometimes trained at the back. In the early part of the fifteenth century they followed the style of houppelande with high collars.

Mantles, often of silk, were now also being worn as dressing gowns. For outdoor wear they were lavishly lined and fastened with tasselled cords, remaining in fashion throughout the period.

Footwear

Woollen and linen *stockings* were worn and held up by garters either above or below the knees.

Shoe styles were adapted from Oriental fashions brought back by the Crusaders. They were at first made to fit either foot, but by the thirteenth century they were better shaped to the individual foot, and fastened with buckles or by lacing. Pointed shoes became popular in about 1360, but the points were not as pronounced as those of the men. *Buskins* or boots were only worn for riding or travelling, and *galoshes* as well as wooden *pattens*, with leather cross straps over the instep, were worn as protection against inclement weather.

The high-waisted gown has a full skirt. The V-shaped neck opening is filled in with a contrasting material. The tall hennin, shown here, was less popular than the shorter truncated version. Fifteenth century

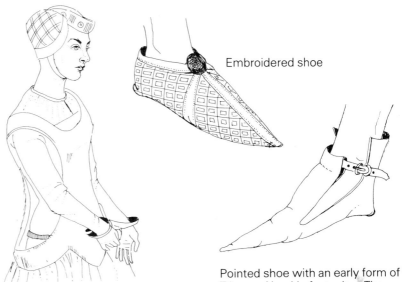

Embroidered shoe

The sleeveless surcote is worn over a long tight sleeved kirtle. The crespine headdress is decorated with a jewelled band. Late fourteenth century

Pointed shoe with an early form of T bar and buckle fastening. The sides low cut and the back high

13

Wimple and veil worn with a goffered front, *c* 1325

The veil is goffered in front, *c* 1370

Decorated padded roll headwear with a short veil hanging behind, *c* 1393

Hair plaited on top of the head and covered with a fine veil, *c* 1450

Headwear and hairstyles

The *barbette* or *wimple* became popular when it was introduced in the reign of Henry II (1133-89). This consisted of a long white linen band worn under the chin to frame the face, and over the top of the head. A small veil or crown was sometimes worn over it. Pleated fillets or headbands, made of either stiff linen or of silk, were worn over the wimple. The hair was usually concealed beneath the veils, although young girls could wear their hair uncovered. In the thirteenth century headwear remained basically the same. The wimple and veil remaining fashionable from the twelfth to the fourteenth century. The material was worn under the chin, with the ends pinned to the hair on either side.

Small caps and coifs were worn in various styles. A *crespine* or *caul* was also worn. This was usually of silk or gold and silver decorated with jewels and was baglike, enclosing the hair.

Young girls wore their hair at least shoulder length and parted in the centre, often plaited with ribbons or encased in silk tubes called *fouriaux*. *Diadems* or circlets were popular with this style.

Fillets adorned with jewellery developed into the crespine which later developed into a fashionable headdress with cylindrical pieces shaped in flexible wire worn either side of the head, joined with a headband. The loose or plaited hair was placed through the cylinder tops, and then hung down in front of the ears.

A ram's horn style was also popular. This consisted of the hair parted in the centre with plaits twisted over the ears and the ends pulled out to form a 'horn'. During the first part of the fourteenth century the wimple was pinned over the plaits with the ends tucked into the bodice.

In the fourteenth century hairstyles were completely covered by the headwear, although hair was plaited and coiled around the ears. Centre partings with horizontal plaits around the head or plaits hanging down were also fashionable by the middle of the century. From about 1380 hair was worn puffed out at the sides covered by nets each side. These were attached to a fillet. The shaven forehead also became popular and remained so until the late fifteenth century.

Wimples and *veils* were still fashionable in the fourteenth century. Veils were often worn alone and shaped into a coif held in place with a fillet. The ends were allowed to hang at the back. A new style of veil, more ornamental, called a goffered veil became fashionable about 1370. It was made of linen in several layers. It was cut semi-circular, the front edge ornamented and frilled, framing the face. Ornamental fillets with side pieces resembling pillars gave a square-faced effect. The hair was drawn through the pillars. Vertical plaited hair could replace these pillar-like fillets.

Towards the end of the fourteenth century the chaplet style was popular, worn over a fret or caul. Hair remained covered beneath a veil, although it was coiled or braided around the ears.

In the early fifteenth century headdresses became even more elaborate. Hair was often shaved off above the forehead and the remaining hair concealed beneath the headwear. Wide shapes with side attachements, known as *templars*, just above the ears, enclosed the hair. They were often made in gold and encrusted with jewels.

Linen head covering with wimple, *c* 1470

U-shaped decorative rolled headdress, *c* 1460

Purse and keys suspended from a belt. Fourteenth century

Nets were worn beneath the fillets and draped at the back. The width of the templars depended on the prevailing fashion. They became extremely wide by about 1416, developing into horned headdress. Fine veils or nets were entwined, the ends falling loose in folds at the back. As the horns increased in size, they formed a U shape above the forehead.

Towards the end of the fifteenth century it became fashionable to pluck the eyebrows as well as to shave the forehead.

Headwear became even higher. The templars were seen less often, and a V shape roll arched from the forehead up either side was worn, tilted to the back, with a *gorget* and sometimes a liripipe. By the end of the century these horned type styles were replaced by a French style of steeple-shaped truncated *hennin* which resembled an inverted flower pot, and was also worn tilted to the rear. A small black loop or frontlet was attached to the centre front to enable the headdress to be adjusted correctly. These headdresses were covered with long flowing veils, either attached from the front or draped over the hennin. As many of the veils were ground length, they were then carried over one arm, in similar fashion to a trained dress. After about 1470 a broad black band of material was attached over the front, with the ends hanging to shoulder level either side.

Butterfly headdress styles were popular during the second half of the fifteenth century. They were of transparent gauze on a wire frame over the truncated hennin. The wire frame was shaped into a V with the dip in the front. When, towards the end of the century, the truncated hennin became shorter, the headdress evolved into the Tudor style of bonnet. Veils became narrower and longer with the ends knotted to keep them off the ground. Also in the late 1400s an open circular headdress allowed the hair to be worn long, eminating from the centre opening.

Accessories

Large *aprons* without bibs and tied around the waist were mainly worn in the country for working in the fields and for spinning. These could be embroidered. They were also worn for domestic chores.

Gloves were being worn by all classes of the fourteenth century, richly embroidered and encrusted with jewels. Glove makers were recorded as early as 1295.

Decorative jewellery in all forms as well as ornamental girdles were popular. Red and white roses were the most fashionable decorative motifs used during the Lancastrian and Yorkist (1399-1483) period.

Wide headdress with templars, *c* 1420

Horned headdress with wimple, *c* 1430

Sixteenth century

The fitted bodice had a wide low square neckline edged with a narrow frill. The long skirt open in front, displayed the decorative kirtle. The wide fur-trimmed cuffs on the sleeves of the overgarment had long decorative undersleeves attached with buttons or ties. The hair, parted in the centre, is coiled at the back, hidden by the French hood, *c* 1535

The voluminous sleeves are turned back to reveal the lining. The yoke and false sleeves are both in the same colour. The turned back collar and wrist frills are lace edged. Around the neck is a pendant. Hanging from the girdle and held in the hand is a small prayer book

Women's dress did not alter greatly until 1495 when the Renaissance and Tudor period made a significant impression. The most typical form of dress was the *gown* and *kirtle*.

The kirtle was worn over a chemise or undergarment. Until the middle of the sixteenth century the bodice and skirt were usually joined. The full conical skirt was generally fastened in the front at the waist, and revealed an underskirt of a contrasting colour. The neckline varied, but square necklines were becoming fashionable. The front was cut to an arch over the bosom, and the décolletage filled in with a high necked chemise, or a stomacher or a *partlet*, usually without a collar until about 1530 when narrow and frilled collars were added.

After about 1525 the bodice became closer fitting and slightly stiffened, and the waistline slightly dipped in the front. The kirtle also became more elaborate and was worn without a gown. The neckline was wide and square in the front, and formed a V shape at the back. The edges were richly embroidered with jewels and lace.

The gown worn with a kirtle was voluminous, usually made in one. In the early part of the century it was high waisted and the bodice was close fitting with the skirt full from the hips and hanging to the ground with a long train, in heavy folds, often hitched to the waist and fastened with a brooch, tucked into the girdle at the waist, or carried over the arm revealing the coloured lining. However, after about 1540 the train became less fashionable, and the skirt, still full and gathered at the waist, became slightly shorter. A gored skirt in a cone shape, without the extra fullness from waist to hem, became popular. The inverted V shape in the front revealed the embroidered and decorative skirt or kirtle, which became known as the petticoat. In the second part of the century skirts of the gown were often caught up at the sides to reveal the richly embroidered underskirts.

The low neckline was square in front with a V shape at the back. It was either laced or fastened with hooks and eyes in the front to the waist. The décolletage was covered by the bodice of the kirtle or chemise. The sleeves, close fitting from the shoulder, widened into a funnel shape towards the wrists where a deep turned-back cuff revealed a fur or contrasting coloured lining.

From about 1535 a close fitting bodice of the gown dipped into a deep point, revealing the bodice underneath the neckline, high or low, and had a low stand-up collar called a *Medici*. The low cut bodices, sometimes

Deep pointed bodice with a low neckline and an embroidered edge, *c* 1592

down to the waist, were regarded as a symbol of virginity in Tudor times – high closed bodices being evidence of the marital status. Queen Elizabeth I invariably wore extremely low-cut bodices.

The bodice and skirt were separate from about mid century. The bodice, called 'a pair of bodies' by the Elizabethans, was a stiff corset-like garment supported by whalebone, metal or wood stays known as *busks*.

Doublets, similar to those worn by men, were worn in place of the bodice of the kirtle.

To almost the end of the century the close-fitting bodice ended in a short point at the waistline, closing on the left side with hooks and eyes. After about 1580 the close fitting bodice became longer in the waist. The front was in a deep V opening with the edges embroidered. This embroidery could be narrow at the base, increasing to the shoulders, forming a flat turned-down collar. This low neckline demanded a stomacher front. The stomacher was attached to the bodice by ties, hidden on the inside of the edge. Ruffs were always worn; the popular large cartwheel ruff was sometimes wired for support.

The high neck of the chemise with its frilled standing collar and small V necked opening filled in the décolletage. When the chemise was discarded about 1560 the décolletage was exposed with just a small neck ruff. A partlet or 'fill-in' could be worn with a standing collar. This was generally in a contrasting colour to the bodice and decorated with semi-precious stones. However, the colour of the partlet matched that of the sleeves. From the 1560s a high standing collar and separate ruff was worn. A large closed cartwheel ruff became fashionable in the 1570s.

Funnel shaped sleeves remained fashionable until 1560s. They were tight-fitting to the elbows and ended with a wide turned-back cuff in front and a hanging streamer behind. The undersleeve, tight at the wrist, was revealed by the wide oversleeve and could be slashed. The frilled cuff of the chemise was visible at the wrist.

From about 1560 the close-fitting sleeves were slightly bombasted and decorated with slashes and puffs of the chemise protruding, as did the chemise wrist ruff. There were many varieties of sleeve. They could be slashed and puffed, full or well fitting at the shoulders. Sometimes shoulder welts or wings were favoured. The hanging sleeves popular until about 1560 later became sham. Puffed out sleeves with deep cuffs at the elbows had detachable sleeves, fitting close to the wrist attached. Another popular style of sleeve was full from the shoulders to the wrist where it ended with a close-fitting cuff and hand ruff. Another style often seen, had a fullness which balanced the width of the *farthingale*.

Towards the latter part of the century sleeves became large and bombasted, the full sleeves becoming even fuller with padding. A demi-cannon sleeve was also stiffened with buckram and wire or whalebone, and could be slashed. Turned-back lace cuffs and small hand ruffs were also seen.

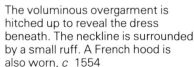

The voluminous overgarment is hitched up to reveal the dress beneath. The neckline is surrounded by a small ruff. A French hood is also worn, *c* 1554

Spanish style farthingale, *c* 1550

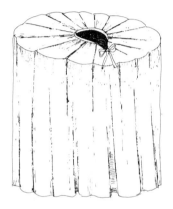

French style farthingale, *c* 1580

Roll farthingale worn around the hips, *c* 1575

Small neck ruff and close fitting coif covering the ears, *c* 1575

Underwear

The farthingale was slowly accepted, it became so popular that it was eventually worn by all classes. It was a circular whalebone frame fastened around the hips and worn as a foundation for petticoats and kirtles. The English farthingale was worn tilted up at the back, giving an unbalanced appearance. When worn with the triangular corset, the whole body was given a pyramid shape. A long body and short legs was another silhouete achieved with these foundation garments.

The first style, the Spanish farthingale, reached England around 1545 and remained popular until 1590, whilst the French farthingale following in about 1580 lasted until the 1620s.

The *Spanish farthingale* was a linen petticoat with horizontal steel or whalebone bands becoming wider from the waist down forming a funnel or dome shape, usually cane spokes supported at the top at the waist, but with the greater part of the circumference at the back. Over this frame were worn two or three voluminous petticoats, an underskirt, and over the entirety, the overdress. The skirt was gored to produce a stiff flat effect from waist to hem. An inverted V shape in the front revealed a plain underskirt, covered by an embroidered forepart.

The *French farthingale*, Queen Elizabeth's favourite, introduced around 1580, consisted of a single padded hoop or a bolster-like pad fastened around the waist sloping from the back to the point of the stomacher. Under this was worn a petticoat and over the pad several more petticoats and then the skirt which was very full, cut circular and gathered at the waist and allowed to fall in many folds.

The *roll farthingale*, also known as a *bum roll*, was a bombasted pad worn around the hips tied together in the front. It was worn to give an upward tilt at the back.

Later, from about 1580 to 1620, a wheel farthingale also known as a *Catherine wheel* or *Italian farthingale* was introduced. The horizontal stiffeners formed around the waist gave a wheel effect and measured about 130 cm (50 in.) across. This was worn with a tilt up at the back. The top of the skirt was box pleated radiating from the waist like the spokes of a wheel and then allowed to fall to the ankles, just revealing the feet. A narrow inverted V opening in the front just revealed the ornamental forepart. To hide the starkness of the hoops, a circular piece of material, ruched to give a ruff effect around the waist, formed horizontal folds which slightly overlapped at the edge. When the wheel farthingale became fashionable corsets were adapted to accentuate the line. Corsets were first introduced in the 1530s and were of wood, iron, leather and perforated steel, flat and triangular. They were designed to flatten the bosom and to give clothes a smooth fit.

Fashionable ladies, as well as men, used a great deal of bombast to emphasise the desired form.

It was in this century that women first began to wear *drawers*, a type of trouser tied at the waist, reaching to the knees and fastened to stockings with garters. They were first made of cotton or fustian, and later of silks and brocades, elegant enough to be allowed to be visible beneath the gowns.

Until Tudor times, underwear was very simple, consisting mainly of a linen shift. Shirts and undershirts or chemises worn beneath kirtles and

Cartwheel ruff. The hair is worn back and slightly built up

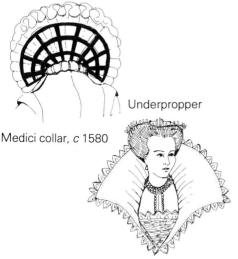

Medici collar, *c* 1580

Underpropper

The gown is worn over a French farthingale. The bodice front comes to a deep point. The bombasted sleeves are slashed and the puffs of the chemise protruded. A close fitting ruff encircled the neck, *c* 1586

overgarments were more elaborate, made of fine linens, embroidered and decorated with jewels, as they could be visible through the slashings of the overgarments.

Night attire

At night most people, especially the not-so-wealthy, slept naked. The wealthier wore *railes* which were a kind of nightgown or shawl. They were generally made like a loose chemise with embroidery around the sleeves and neckline. Small neck and wrist ruffs were often lace edged. A coif made of linen or fustian was worn at night. A triangular piece of material matching the coif and worn with the point either to the front or back, was tied either under the chin or behind, could be worn over the coif.

Neckwear

Neck frills were worn from the mid sixteenth century to give a finish to the collars of the partlets or chemises. This small frill was gradually increased in size until it became a ruff. The giant cartwheel ruff became popular from the 1580s into the seventeenth century, worn with high or low necklines. Ruffs became larger when starch was introduced. During the latter part of the Elizabethan era the width varied from 20-40 cm (9-15 in.) and the full length of the band could not always support the ruffs at the back, so a wire aid known as a *supportasse* or *rebato* was worn, shaped and fastened to a décolletage and filled with several layers of lace-edged material. Small circular ruffs were sometimes worn close to the neck to mark where the large ruff surrounded the neck. They were sometimes worn in more than one layer, even as many as four.

A *headraile*, an adaptation of a shawl, worn around the shoulders and over the head, fashionable from the start of the century, was wired and formed an arch shape over the head from about 1590. The material used was usually diaphanous and lace edged and often starched.

Overgarments

A warm overgarment or *gown* was fashionable until the 1620s. It was close fitting at the shoulders and fell in loose folds to the ground. The front could be left open in an inverted V, thus exposing the underskirt. The collar varied from a high standing to a narrow round shape. Elbow-length sleeves had shoulder puffs; long sleeves were often of the hanging variety with openings at the elbows for the arms to protrude. Armholes were often decorated with welts and rolls, especially if the gown was without sleeves.

Another style fitted closely to the waist and fell in heavy folds to the ground. A ruff or high Medici collar remained popular. Front fastening was with ribbon points or buttons and loops. At hip level there were placket holes edged with embroidery. These were so that the girdle beneath with its various attachments could be reached.

Cloaks were still worn, but mainly for travelling. These were of thick material, with a combined hood. The hood was wired to arch the face, sometimes curving down the centre. The length of the cloak varied from ground to waist.

Square toed shoe with a large ribbon rosette

Square backed chopine with a slashed and cut-out mule attached

English gable hood with lappets pinned up, c 1528

Type of French hood with a fine veil, c 1530

Footwear and legwear

Stockings were mainly of material tailored and cut on the cross for a better fit, reaching above the knees, held up with garters which might, in some cases, extend to ornamental ribbon bands decorated with jewels and gold-lace fringing. Cross-gartered ribbons were also worn. As stockings improved, just an embroidered and buckled band could be worn at the knees.

In 1589 a graduate clergyman from Cambridge, William Lee, invented a stocking frame which enabled stockings to be mechanically knitted, thus making them cheaper and more popular. By 1598 there was a further improvement so that instead of just being able to produce them in worsted or cotton, silk stockings became available, which might also be embroidered with clocks above the ankles.

Shoes similar to the men's were fastened with ornamental buckles or laces. Slashings and cut designs over the rounded toes and insteps were fashionable.

Buskins or high boots, generally of soft leather or velvet were worn mainly for riding.

Chopines or cork clogs covered in leather were worn for extra height as well as to keep the feet from dirty ground. Often they were worn over more delicate shoes, or were all in one piece with the shoes.

In the 1570s a method of fastening shoes with ribbon bows became the vogue, often finished with rosettes resembling flowers.

Pumps, also called *slippers*, came into use in the middle of the sixteenth century with thin soles, and low heels. There were no fastenings and the feet were slipped directly into them.

Headwear

The style and fashions of headwear changed completely from previous times. The hennin and tall headwear was replaced by lower and closer-fitting styles. *Undercaps* were popular, being worn under most headdresses. They were secured with a pin to the hair, or with a strap under the chin. A band or frontlet worn beneath was just visible and could be either goffered or embroidered.

Coifs were worn indoors or under headwear instead of caps. They had a seam across the top, the front being straight or shaped over the forehead to reveal the hair. They were mainly of a decorative or patterned design for day wear, or plain linen or fustian for night attire.

The undercap worn with the French hood always had the edge visible, and this was either pleated or embroidered.

Another type of cap popular from 1525 to about 1580 was the lettice cap. This was triangular in shape, covering the ears, made of lettice – a fur similar to ermine – or of miniver.

Towards the end of the century, lawn caps also became popular; they were of ruching joined to a horseshoe back and beneath them was often worn a triangular kerchief with the point over the forehead. These caps were popular until well into the seventeenth century.

Stiffened hood, c 1530

French hood revealing the fitted cap beneath. The back is raised and the hood allowed to hang behind, c 1540

Close fitting hat decorated with feathers and jewels, c 1548

A version of the French hood. The front piece of velvet curved, ending behind the ears and edged with a band of jewels, behind this is a piece of white material set with precious stones giving a coronet effect. The black hood itself is attached to the crescents and fell down the back in a flat tube-like, c 1550

From about 1558 the taffeta *pipkin* was popular. This was worn over a caul or net made of stiffened taffeta with a pleated crown and narrow brim.

Hats were of varous shapes and sizes, some were flat with narrow brims, others tall and stiff with feather decorations fastened to the hatband with a jewel. A style of bonnet or headdress with a small crown trimmed with contrasting bands and a front band hanging down at the sides was an adaptation of the truncated hennin.

Hoods were also very popular at the start of the century until about 1530. They fell in folds at the shoulders with a slit to ear level, giving two streamers or lappets at the sides, and a curtain effect at the back. The edges could be turned back to reveal the lining and undercap. A wide embroidered band was often placed over this. About 1515 the side lappets became shorter.

The *English hood* or gable headdress worn from the beginning of the century until about 1540, had a characteristically pointed arch of stiffened wire which framed the face. The lappets were turned up at ear level and pinned to the crown. The back curtain was replaced by streamers which could be allowed to hang to almost waist level or also be pinned up.

The back of the hood often formed into a flat diamond shape. A stiff undercap was essential with this style and the side curves fastened under the chin with a narrow band. The hair was hidden in front and the gable front filled with padded rolls of striped silk.

The *Mary Stuart hood* was similar, made of plain stiff linen, shaped around the face with a slight dip over the forehead, curving to just below the cheeks, with folds to the shoulders.

From about 1530 to 1580 a *French hood* style was popular. This was stiff and worn towards the back of the head curving either side over the ears. The back was raised, the hood itself falling down the back. It was made of one piece of black velvet following the shape of the head to the ears, heart shaped, curving outwards towards the sides. This was achieved with a wire shape, an *attifet*, covered by a veil which fell to a point over the forehead. The top edge was ornamented and behind was another band or braid. At the back a coronet was headed by a row of ornamental beads, and in front, resting on the back, a small, shaped white band tapering to ear level. The decorative edges were called *billiments*, the upper decorating the tilted curve at the back of the crown, whilst the nether billiment edged the lower front curve. Attached to the back of the raised crown a rectangular piece of black velvet formed a tube that hung in folds. As neck ruffs increased in size, the fall at the back of the hood was sometimes arranged to turn back over the top, so that it projected over the front, thus shading the face. This was known as a *bongrace*. As hairstyles became more elaborate, high crowned hats became fashionable, expecially for riding. Hatbands were often plaited, or if left flat, encrusted with jewellery or richly embroidered.

Barbes, long pieces of vertically pleated linen were worn under the chin and fastened to the hair at the back with a veil and attifet or hood on the head. These were usually worn by widows or people in mourning. Married women had their heads covered in and out of doors, whilst single girls did not wear hats quite so often.

Headrailes, popular in Elizabethan times were veils encrusted with

The attifet worn with a French hood, the back of which formed a roll from which the flat tube hung down the back. The attifet itself was made of wire inserted into the front edge of the hood forming a curve either side of the forehead with a point in the centre, giving a heart-shaped effect. The partlet or fill-in radiated from the neck and is surmounted by a small ruff, *c* 1555

Mary Stuart hood made of stiff linen, *c* 1561

This style of hat was worn mainly for hunting. The hard crown is shaped like an inverted flower pot covered with silk or brocade and the brim is bound in a braid. The base of the crown is surrounded by beads with ostrich feathers at the back. The hat is worn tilted slightly forward, and with a caul beneath, *c* 1575

jewels and made of transparent materials. They were wired to curve behind the head and fasten to the shoulders.

Hairstyles

As hair was mainly concealed in the earlier part of the century, the hairstyles were kept simple. Hair was generally parted in the centre, and would occasionally hang loosely at the back from underneath the hood. About 1520 when hoods were pinned up, plaited hair was often encased in a striped covering and brought to the front, just visible beneath the gable front of the hood. The side hair was brought slightly forward and puffed. The top hair could be raised a little and the back, coiled at the nape of the neck, often enclosed in an ornamental caul. This was a popular style, especially with the French type of hoods.

There was a great deal of ornamentation; feathers, pendants and brooches were attached to pins or wires and placed in the hair.

Such was the popularity of Queen Elizabeth I, that most fashionable ladies dyed their hair auburn to follow her fashion. Towards the end of the sixteenth century they began to build up their hairstyles in the front to give extra height. This was achieved with quantities of curls and puffs mounted on false hair. Wigs were also worn. Pads raised on wire supports, known as *palisades*, had either real or false hair to give the impression of extra fullness. A slight dip in the front gave a heart-shaped effect.

Hair was plucked at the temples to give a higher forehead.

Accessories

Girdles were a very popular accesory, often long and narrow with tassels or with a jewelled chain from which hung a pomander. Also they could be very ornate and ornamented with precious jewels and metals.

Pomanders were very popular in gold, silver or ivory, jewelled and enamelled. Shapes ranged from circular, square and ballshaped. The filigree perforations allowed the perfume to escape.

As Elizabethan dresses had no pockets, girdles were all-important as they had suspended from them various articles such as leather or material string-drawn purses, large or small fans that were made of feathers with elaborate inlaid handles, mirrors, prayer books or the Book of Hours, or indeed small fur or skin hand muffs were also sometimes suspended from girdles attached by ribbons. *Watches* were also suspended, this being the origin of the Regency fob watch and chain, so popular, especially amongst men.

A short shoulder cape, worn more as a decoration than for warmth, was the *tippet* with a narrow Medici collar.

Neckerchiefs, usually squares of white material were used as fill-ins for low décolletages, as were shawls. *Headrailes*, adaptations of shawls were worn around the shoulders and covered the head.

As jewellery was very large and cumbersome in Elizabethan times, scent could also be carried in rings, necklaces and pendants.

Gloves were mainly of velvets, satins or silks, except for riding, when they were leather or doeskin. They had either large cuffs or gauntlets which were richly embroidered. Gloves with *cuttes* around the fingers allowed for the large rings to protrude. Sweet or perfumed gloves known

Cap made of a trellis of puffs with a horseshoe shaped back. The front has a shaped piece of lawn edged with narrow pleated ruching and wired like an attifet to curve over the hair which is dressed in small curls. Beneath the cap is worn a triangular kerchief with the point on the forehead, c 1584

as *frangipani* gloves were also very fashionable. Embroidered mittens were worn towards the end of the century.

Aprons were a fashionable accessory by the wealthier, made of silks and taffetas, often lace-trimmed. The lower classes wore aprons mainly for domestic purposes, and these were of heavier and more practical materials.

Lace-edged embroidered *handkerchiefs* were carried. These were fringed and tasselled and made in delicate materials such as lawns and silks.

Mufflers became fashionable in the 1550s for the wealthy and became more commonplace during Queen Elizabeth's reign. They were a type of headscarf covering the lower part of the face in cold weather and fastening at the back. They were of velvet or sable for the upper classes.

Also from about the 1550s *masks* were worn by men, as well as women, for secrecy and coquetry as well as for protection against dust and sun – sun tans being very unfashionable in this time. They covered the entire face and were held on by a silver or glass button held between the teeth like a horse's bit. Masks usually made from skins, silks or satins, were in various shapes, but there were always holes for the eyes. A loo mask (a term derived from the French word 'loup' a wolf) was a half mask, also used for protection.

Pomander

The hair is parted in the centre and worn off the forehead, puffed or waved at the sides, so filling out the sides of the French hood. The hair at the back could be coiled to fit into a network caul of goldsmith's work embroidered with jewels

Glove with cuttes around the fingers, c 1550

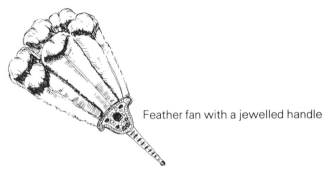

Feather fan with a jewelled handle

The high waisted dress with the square-edged décolletage has a full loose skirt. The full sleeves were also lace edged, *c* 1625

Open robe with a stomacher, the bodice ends in a rounded point in front. The open gown revealed the petticoat in front, *c* 1664

Seventeenth century

Formal Elizabethan dress was still worn in the early part of the reign of James I (1603-1625) and was only gradually influenced by French fashions. Bombast and stiffness, farthingales and stomachers, were cast aside as softer materials and looser fitting garments became the mode. Higher waistlines and more pronounced décolletages became popular; lace and ribbons replaced the heavy precious stones and elaborate embroidery of the previous era.

Changes began to occur in the second half of the century. Although still basically the same, dress consisted of bodice, petticoat and gown. The gown that had previously been mainly an overgarment became an integral part of the costume from about 1625.

In the first part of the century the bodice was always worn with a farthingale, but by about 1625, the farthingale was worn less, until it was finally discarded. The bodice and skirt were separate items until about 1680. During this time the high waistline had a slight point in front whilst the bodice was close fitting with a low décolletage and stiffened with busks. These were generally of wood or metal, or, for the wealthy, of carved ivory. They were worn to push up the breasts.

The bodice was closed in the front with lacing, ribbon bow ties or buttons. Over the bodice was worn a stomacher which was a stiff triangular piece of canvas with the point to the waist. This was generally straight at the top and covered with a material that matched the sleeves but was in contrast to the bodice itself. This was worn to cover the fastening of the bodice and was usually very decorative. *Echelles* or rows of ribbon bows were considered very elegant.

The low décolletage remained fashionable, especially for the unmarried. Married women usually filled the low décolletage with a shirt or chemise that had a high lace-edged collar. A lace *bertha* or shawl of fine material could also cover the low décolletage.

The sleeves of the bodice followed earlier styles, cannon sleeves being popular until the 1620s. These were gathered at the shoulders tapering towards the wrists where they ended with a small ruff or lace cuff. These sleeves were often padded at the top or stiffened with wire or whalebone. Wings at the shoulders often covered the join of the sham hanging sleeves. Sleeves varied, some being full to the elbows revealing the chemise sleeves, others with the top seam left open to allow the chemise sleeves to

PLATE 1 Front left *The overtunic embroidered around the edge is worn over a long undertunic. The veil is draped around the shoulders and neck. Norman period, c 1135.* Back left *The low bodice is filled in with a partlet, and the long full sleeves are caught just above the elbows with a band matching the rest of the embroidery, c 1539.* Foreground *The sideless surcoat is worn over a kirtle with long tight sleeves. The caul, either side, is surrounded by plaits and surmounted with a decorative roll, c 1400.* Right *The high ruff is wired at the back leaving a low décolletage in front. The long sleeves end with lace cuffs matching the ruff. The French farthingale was popular, c 1600*

PLATE 2   Far left *The dress is in the high-waisted Empire style worn with a redingote with a cape-like collar. The tall bonnet is decorated with drooping ostrich feathers, c 1810.* Left *The stiff-crowned hat with a wide brim is decorated with a hatband and feathers. The hair is frizzed. The décolletage of the dress is filled in with a neckerchief, c 1785.*   Right *The high and narrow fontange headdress consists of a small cap* wired with ribbons and lace. The long ends hang down. Around the neck is a Steinkirk cravat. The front of the petticoat is decorated, c 1693.   Far right *The lady wears a chaperon headdress and a cape. The overskirt is gathered and bunched up at the back revealing a skirt beneath. A large fur muff is carried, c 1640*

Stiffened corset with lacing at the back, c 1625

Corset stiffened with whalebone, laced at the back and a decorated false front, c 1660

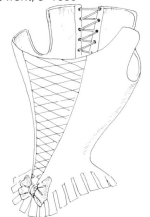

Quilted bodice, laced at the back, c 1670

Plain tabbed bodice stiffened with cane or whalebone

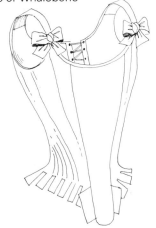

emerge. Other variations included wide or narrow sleeves ending at the elbows and lined with lace falls.

Jackets, similar to those of the doublets worn by men with basques or tabs at the waist, remained popular in the first quarter of the century, sometimes worn in place of the bodice. They were close fitting and slightly stiffened, flaring out at the waist, the skirts ending at about hip level. They were generally collarless with a deep V-shaped opening in the front, fastened with buttons, hooks and eyes or ribbon ties. The straight, tight-fitting sleeves always ended with small cuffs that could be turned back, and a hand-ruff.

Farthingales remained fashionable until the 1620s. To accentuate the tilt a bum roll could be worn. This latter was then worn alone, giving the skirt a tub shaped effect. Skirts still had the inverted V opening in the front.

It also became popular to follow the earlier style (1590s) of bunching up the sides of the skirts to reveal the embroidered petticoats.

Later the skirts were pleated at the waist, falling to the ground, still with an inverted V opening in front exposing the decorated underskirts. The edges of the overskirts could be either pulled up or turned back and fastened.

About mid-century the backs of the skirts became trained, and by the 1680s were extremely long. These trains could be pulled up behind to give a bustle effect – this was in fact the early type of bustle.

Underwear

In the seventeenth century *corsets* were plain in the front, lacing at the back so that the diaphram was flattened and the bosom pushed even higher than previously. *Petticoats* were cut similarly to the skirts, also slightly trained when that mode became fashionable, but cut slightly shorter in the front, to just above the ankles. They were generally very decoratively embroidered and later trimmed with lace flounced at the hem or hip level.

Gowns

Gowns as overgarments remained popular until the 1620s gradually becoming old-fashioned although still worn by the elderly until the 1640s. They were loose fitting to the ground and could be fastened all the way down with buttons and loops, or left open. They could also be worn with just the top fastened or with just a sash around the waist. Necklines varied from small standing collars or revers and lapels forming a V opening. Wings were always present, even when the gowns were sleeveless. Sometimes only hanging sleeves were in evidence, although short straight sleeves were also seen. When not worn as an overgown outdoors, but as a négligé in the home, they had long sleeves. Until the 1650s, when gowns referred to whole costumes, the bodices were short waisted with basques or tabs, similar to the male doublets, but fastening could be front or back. Front fastening was from eyelet holes in the flaps attached to the bodice by lacing. Stomachers were always present with a rounded tab centre front that sloped down. When fastened at the back, the neckline was usually high allowing for a low décolletage in the front. This was usually fastened with hooks and eyes or lacing, and the wealthier even used jewelled

Small fan-shaped ruff worn with a low décolletage. The turned back cuffs matched the ruff. The full skirt is hidden in front by a long apron. The coif is close fitting with points over the ears, *c* 1630

(a) Heeled shoe of soft pleated leather fastened with a wide strap and buckle. Early seventeenth century. (b) Flat shoe with a large rosette over the fastening. Early seventeenth century. (c) Square-toed, low-heeled shoe fastened with a large ribbon bow. Early to mid-seventeenth century. (d) Riding boot with elastic gusset, *c* 1655. (e) Pantoffle with a double sole. (f) Quilted mule decorated with a frill a the top

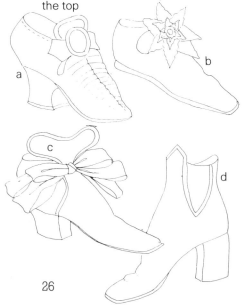

clasps. Stomachers were not usual with back closures, although false ones might be worn. Basques were not always present, but the bodices, tight fitting to the waist, came to a point in the front and a narrow ribbon belt followed the contours of the waistline. Until the 1640s sleeves were full, ballooned and paned, or they could be short, exposing the chemise sleeve beneath. The gown skirts were gathered at the waist falling to ground level. Centre openings were seen, but closed skirts became popular until the 1650s. These were known as *fitted bodice gowns*. The older styles worn as overgarments were sometimes incorporated into the newer fashions.

By the 1680s the joined bodice and skirt gowns were fashionable. The bodice was fairly close fitting attached to a fully trained skirt, often hitched up and the centre front open to reveal the petticoat. The bodice was often with a deep V opening in the front that was filled in by an embroidered stomacher. Sleeves were generally elbow length with turned-up cuffs. By the 1690s lace frills were attached to the cuffs instead of revealing the chemise sleeves.

Neckwear and wristwear

Ruffs, collars and falling bands remained popular throughout the first part of the century. All types of ruffs were worn with high or low necklines, but the fan-shaped ruffs only with low décolletages. A later style of neckwear included a *bertha*, fashionable from about 1625-1650, which consisted of a lace or diaphanous material surrounding a low décolletage, meeting in the front, similar to a neckerchief. This could be fastened with a jewelled clasp. *Gorgets* or *whisks*, deep falling cape-like collars were worn from the second half of the seventeenth century into the 1690s.

From the late 1690s the Steinkirk *cravats* were fashionable. They were generally of lawn, lace edged and loosely knotted beneath the chin, pinned to the left side of the bodice. The fashion and name derived from the Battle of Steinkirk in 1692 . They were usually worn with riding habits.

Hand ruffs were still very fashionable in the first quarter of the century, but were gradually susperseded by laced turned-back cuffs attached to sleeves. Frills and lace often matched that of the neckwear.

Cloaks and coats

Cloaks remained popular for wear in cold and bad weather. They were ground length and fastened at the neck with ties or cords, fastening further down with buttons. They were often lined with warm materials as well as fur. *Tippets* or short capes might also be added for additional warmth.

Short, hip-length loose-fitting *coats*, as well as long ones with wide sleeves, were worn. From the 1680s tippets were also worn over coats, the cape gradually becoming smaller to form a deep collar.

Footwear and legwear

Until the 1630s all shoes and boots were fairly rounded in the toes, later becoming more squared. Soles were of cork or leather, cork being used to raise the soles. Heels became popular in the 1600s. The early heels were low, but they became more shaped and elegant as they became higher.

Shoe roses were a common form of decorative trimming. They were made of ribbon loops, lace or leather, becoming large and elaborate.

Standing band collar and sugar loaf shaped hat with a plaited hatband and feather decoration, c 1616

Mary Stuart hat. Early seventeenth century

Fontange headdress, basically a small linen cap with tall pleated and stiffened lace tiers with side lappets and ribbon bows at the sides, c 1690

Boots were generally reserved for horse riding and were made of soft leathers, close fitting, fastening up at the sides.

Pantoffles were a type of overshoe or mule worn in good road conditions, and were similar in design to chopines and pattens. They were decorative and ornamental and could have scenes painted on them. Chopines and pattens were entirely separate from shoes and were secured by leather straps.

It was only in the Restoration period that shoe fashions altered. The styles became more pointed and high Louis heels with the curved fronts gave shoes a more delicate appearance. They were often fastened in front with buckled straps. Materials varied from leather to brocades and silks, often embroidered. *Slippers*, worn indoors, were dainty and might be made of quilted materials. They were often lace-cuffed around the ankles and embroidered.

Stockings were made in a variety of colours and were almost always knitted.

Headwear

Head coverings were generally worn less and less.

The French hood with the back turned up over the front as a bongrace became smaller and was worn further to the back with the front slightly peaked. The Mary Stuart fashion, so popular in the previous century, remained a favourite at the start of the seventeenth century. The Mary Stuart hood was usually of white lawn, its wide border stiffened with starch or wire and trimmed with lace. The sides stood out, but the hood itself was close fitting with the back hanging piece adaptable to a bongrace. These fashions were most popular with the elderly. From about the mid 1620s an unstiffened version made of fine material became more popular.

Long *hoods*, often to ground length wired to arch over the forehead and extend over the face remained in fashion from the Elizabethan era into the first half of the seventeenth century. They were curved in at the neckline or waist and draped like a cape. They were worn mainly outdoors or for mourning. Young widows often wore slightly stiffened thin veils instead. After mid-century they became softer, draped with the front forming a peak at the forehead. Shorter veils were worn in the summer to protect the face from the sun.

Coifs were still worn mainly by the middle class. They were close fitting with a seam on top, and decorated with embroidery. They were fastened with a string at the neck edge. Worn beneath hats and for informal wear, they alleviated the necessity for elaborate hairstyles but by about 1660 they were made to fit over the more elegant hair fashions, with a band at the back so that extra material could be gathered at the crown. Linen, lace-edged coifs, known as *cornets*, fitted the back of the head, and had lappets or streamers down each side.

To accommodate the taller hairstyles of the 1640s soft hoods were made of double material with the front folded back to frame the face.

As the tall hairstyles continued in fashion, reaching extreme heights in the 1690s, the fontange headdress came into fashion. This was basically a small linen cap worn at the back of the head with pleated and stiffened tiers of linen or lace pleated in the front. These tiers were supported by a wire

Lace edged and embroidered coif or cornet, *c* 1623

Coif with short lappets

The ringlets wired to stand away from the face and a pleated bun at the back, *c* 1660

Hair with short fringe in front and the remainder brushed back with the sides puffed out and frizzed, *c* 1620

frame known as a *commode*. Two long linen lappets hanging behind were often pinned up to the crown at the sides. Ribbon knots could be used as ornamentation. For outdoor wear silk hoods, tied in the front, were draped over the cap. These soft hoods were known as chaperones, and were popular until the end of the century.

Hats similar to the Elizabethan styles were mainly worn for travelling or riding. Tall crowned hats with turned-up brims were popular amongst the upper class. They often had plaited or twisted hatbands and were decorated with plumes and jewels. Sugarloaf shaped hats were worn more by the middle class.

In the first quarter of the century lower-crowned hats with wide brims were worn in a variety of styles. These were generally referred to as Cavalier styles. Country women wore hats over linen coifs which were often pulled down at the sides and fashioned with ribbons under the chin.

Hairstyles

The tall hairstyles continued to be fashionable in the first part of James I reign (1566-1625). The hair, high in the front, was still placed over pads or curved wire frames. The back was either in a bun or in thin plaits. *Cauls* or nets with ornamental edgings were still worn and for decoration ribbon bows or plumes were popular. Sometimes just a single ornament was worn, such as a jewelled pin shaped into a crescent or star. False hair or wigs were also still popular. By about 1614 the tall hairstyles were superseded by lower fashions with the hair brushed back from the forehead and puffed out at the sides. The wire supports became completely unfashionable, but pads were still used, mainly to give the fullness. The hair at the back was still generally in a bun, whilst the sides became shorter. Jewelled ornamentation was replaced with short feathers or bunches of ribbon bows.

During the reign of Charles I (1625-1649) hairstyles altered radically, especially from about 1625, with the hair being parted on both sides, and allowed to fall in ringlets. The centre front hair was pulled back and formed into a flat bun at the back. A small fringe or small curls on the forehead was also popular. Instead of a bun at the back, hair was braided and entwined with pearls or ribbon bows with drooping feathers at the back.

In the 1640s the side curls became longer and the hair hung in ringlets. As the hair generally was parted on both sides just above the ears, the rest of the hair was combed straight back into a large bun decorated with ribbon bows, jewels and feathers or a small caul.

Puritan ladies had their short hair brushed back, or had a centre parting, whilst the Cavalier ladies allowed their hair to grow long with masses of curls or ringlets to the shoulders with ribbon bows and jewels entwined in the hair. Just previous to the Restoration of Charles II in 1660 hairstyles generally became shorter to just below ear level and waved at the sides. From the 1660s the hairstyles became much wider with a centre parting. False curls were added to give a puffed-out effect, and for about ten years the side hair was wired to give extra width to the ringlets that hung either side of the face. The front hair was brushed back to form a bun at the back. In the 1670s wiring became less fashionable and the ringlets fell over the shoulders with just an occasional curl over the forehead.

Tight-fitting gloves almost reaching the elbow-length sleeves which are full and puffed, ending with lace cuffs. The high waisted bodice has the skirt part divided into tabs, similar to a male doublet, *c* 1630

A half-mask and a chaperon were worn as well as the hand muffs and fur collar over the gown with a bertha, *c* 1644

A fashionable hairstyle that originated in Paris and known as a *Hurluberlu*, consisted of masses of close curls in rows over the head, with the hair at the back in a bun, and ringlets falling over the shoulders and nape of the neck. In the 1680s when hairstyles again became higher in the front with hair ornamentation, the centre partings allowed for curls to hang down the sides. In the 1690s the tall hairstyles were again supported by padded rolls and wire known as a *palisade*. The hair was sometimes arranged in peaks either side of a centre parting. This type of hairstyle called a *Tour*, was decorated with ribbon knots or a large bow and fell in loose ringlets. A great deal of false hair was used.

Curls were popular and were known by a variety of names such as *confidantes* when by the ears, *favourites* on either side of the forehead, and *crève-coeurs* for those at the nape of the neck. These curls were created with the use of curling irons or papers and set with gum arabic.

Accessories

Aprons, usually of fine transparent materials and lace-edged were worn as ornamentation at home by fashionable ladies. Plain white ones were more usual amongst the working class.

Gauntlet gloves were mainly worn until the 1630s with the gauntlet part made of six to eight pieces ending in a fringe or scalloped edges. *Plain gloves* made of soft leather often had turned-down cuffs. *Wrist gloves* were often ornamented with lace or ribbon loops, whilst long close-fitting elbow-length gloves, usually of silk or soft leather, were worn on formal occasions. *Scented gloves* continued to be popular.

For summer wear, *mittens* in silk or lace were popular. They were sometimes embroidered. *Muffs*, at the beginning and again towards the end of the century were not very large, but reached their largest proportions in about the 1640s when they were generally worn suspended by a cord around the neck. The smaller ones were carried in the hand.

Scarves and *mufflers* were worn in winter for extra warmth. Fine lace-edged *handkerchiefs* ornamented at the corners with buttons or tassels became less popular after the Restoration, with plain lawn or linen lace-edged handkerchiefs gaining in popularity. Large painted or feather *fans* with decorative handles were popular. These could be perfumed. Also, still fashionable, were *masks*. They were made of velvet, silk or satin and could cover the entire face, and were used as a protection against inclement weather as well as a disguise.

Cosmetics were much used in the Stuart period. They were similar to those used in the previous century – white chalk as powder and lip dyes and rouge. *Plumpers* made of cork were often placed inside the mouth to fill out the cheeks. False eyebrows made of mouse skin were sometimes worn.

Face patches, to hide skin blemishes were worn, sometimes as many as fifteen at a time. These could be in a variety of shapes, such as circles, crescents and stars.

Jewellery remained popular, oval pearls being fashionable for both earrings and hair ornaments.

Back view of a sac back hitched up, with a large apron in front. The high fontange type cap is put over hair worn up, *c* 1780

Open robe with the skirt at the back slightly padded. The front of the bodice is concealed by a large cross-over kerchief. The sleeves are tight fitting. The large hat is profusely decorated with trimmings, *c* 1792

Eighteenth century

As in the previous century, attire still consisted of a petticoat, a bodice and skirt joined to form a gown, although skirts and bodices could be separate. Separate bodices were like jackets and were worn over skirts.

Skirts were often worn open to reveal the decorated petticoat underneath, the shape changing – bustles being popular until about 1710, and again from about 1775, hoops being in vogue in the years between. Hooped skirts remained in fashion for Court wear until the 1820s.

Bodices were nearly always short-sleeved and low décolletages were the mode. There were two types of gown; an open robe, open in front to reveal the petticoat, and the closed fashion which did not require such an ornate petticoat.

Open robe

In the open robe style the bodice was joined to the skirt. Until about 1710 the bodice was long waisted and boned to give a close fit. The front of the bodice was invariably open and edged with sewn-down revers, known as *robings*. These eminated from the back of the neck, over the shoulders and ended at the centre, waist level, giving a V-shaped effect. The robings were quite plain, except for Court wear, until about 1745 when they became more ornate. The front opening was covered with either an underbodice, a stomacher, or a corset. Underbodices were generally sleeveless, worn like a stomacher, but laced at the back. Stomachers were triangular, stiffened or padded fill-ins, the top part straight, achieving a square neckline with the robings down either side. The base was usually pointed, rounded or scalloped. Stomachers could be very ornate, heavily embroidered, or have a row of bows decreasing in size from the décolletage to the waist. These were known as *echelles*.

Stomachers were generally pinned to tabs that were present beneath the robings whilst the plainer styles were attached by cross lacings and often covered by a large neckerchief to the waist which could have a breast knot, or attached with a ribbon band which crossed the robings.

The corset type fill-in was laced at the back underneath the bodice, generally plainer with just a little embroidery.

Open robe with a sac back. The kerchief fill-in is held in place with a bow and the tight sleeves end in flounces. Under the Bergère hat an undercap was worn, c 1755

Open robe with a closed bodice, the décolletage being covered in with a buffon, c 1784

In the 1720s less robings were seen; the bodices were closed with buttons down the front to the waist and had rounded décolletage. Bodice sleeves ending with short cuffs around the elbows were gathered or pleated at the shoulders. From about 1740 the cuffs became larger and fuller, bell shaped, and were stiffened to stand away from the arms. They were narrower towards the bend of the elbow to allow for easier movement. The sleeve opening was wide enough for the chemise sleeve with its frills to protrude. From about 1750 the sleeves became tighter fitting. The flounces or full cuffs were still wide on the outer edge, and extra ruffles were sewn in, the lace edging on these matching that of the lace on the headwear and around the neckline.

The overskirt was attached to the bodice all round, and open in the front in an inverted V to the robings. In the early part of the century the overskirt was trained and worn over a bustle, pleated to the bodice at the back, with the front smooth. From about 1710 until the 1780s dome-shaped hoops were worn to distend the skirts, and for a brief while from about 1713 to the 1740s when they were oval. In the 1760s the hoops became wide to the extreme.

Around 1730 another style became fashionable. The panels either side of the back seam of the tight-fitting bodice converged towards the waist and were continued to expand into the skirt to the hemline. This style became typical and remained throughout the century, being known as a *corsage en fourreau*.

For skirts to hang evenly with oblong hoops or panniers they had to be pleated to the bodice from the robings in front and from the fourreau behind, up to the side seam from whence it continued at the sides in a horizontal seam. The pleating continued on these horizontal seams which were partially left open at the waist, forming placket holes through which a pocket could be reached. Petticoats worn beneath the overskirts were generally of a different colour and elaborately embroidered. For Court wear they were often flounced.

If worn over dome-shaped hoops the petticoats were pleated on to a waistband, tied either at the back or on each side leaving an opening for the pockets to be reached. When worn with pannier styles they were left unpleated with the waistband tied either side.

The *robe a l'Anglaise* worn until the 1780s had a fourreau back. The open bodice, similar to that worn with a sac gown could have robings and a stomacher fill-in. If the robings were not present, the bodice was then closed at the top, sloping to an inverted V leaving the base at the waist open; a false waistcoat or *zone* was worn. The zone could be scalloped or vandyked. A falling collar with edging to match came to the tip of the inverted triangle in the front. Another style, a plain closed bodice with edge to edge fastening was without robings and could end either straight or rounded at the waist. The fourreau back fitted to the waistline with sewn-down pleats converging and then allowed to hang loosely. These styles often had strips of cane sewn into the bodice to stiffen them.

From about 1780 open robes had a higher waistline than previously, and the long full skirts were padded out at the back with bustles, the bodices puffed out in front with a buffon. These gowns were plainer than they had previously been. The bodice with the extremely low décolletage was filled in with a large buffon and decorated with ribbon knots, as could be the

Sac gown, also known as a Watteau gown. The front of the bodice is closed with lacing. A small cap is worn over the simple short hairstyle, c 1730

Closed gown style. The low rounded décolletage is edged with lace and the long tight sleeves buttoning at the wrist are also edged with lace. The front fastening is with buttons down to the hem and a sash with a large bow at the back, c 1780

point at the back of the bodice and the sleeves. There were no robings present and fastenings were in the usual variety of ways, diverging to the waist in an inverted V, the opposite of previous styles.

A waistcoat or zone could also cover the gap of the inverted V opening of the bodice. The shorter sleeves ended with either round cuffs or frills whilst the long tight sleeves buttoned at the wrist, also ending with small frills.

Long wide sashes tied at the back or to one side were very popular, as also were girdles or ribbon belts with jewelled buckles.

The trained overskirts were closely pleated to the bodice, following the curve down at the rear, and in front revealed the long petticoat beneath. Although bustles were not unusual under petticoats, small hoops were also seen. The open robe was worn with variations such as the back en fourreau, or long trains, various methods of distending as well as alternative styles of bodices and decoration were also seen. Sleeves could also be of a different colour to the main garment.

Closed robe

A popular style of gown worn in the first half of the eighteenth century was known as a *wrapping gown* and was of the closed robe style.

The close fitting bodice had a low, rounded décolletage and was without robings. The low neckline was filled in with a *tucker* or modesty piece. The front of the bodice was crossed over like a wrap and in one with the skirt. The front could be closed with an ornamental brooch and a girdle worn around the waist. The sleeves were similar to the open robe styles with several ruffles at the cuffs. Hoops of all sizes could be worn beneath the skirts.

From the 1730s an edge to edge closure was popular and the bodice remained similar to the wrapping gown, often with a modesty piece set in. The closure of the bodice was often with hooks and eyes. The back was joined to the skirt in *corsage en fourreau* fashion, with extra pleating to give more fullness. Another closed robe form was the *sac*. In the early 1720s this was rather a shapeless gown with box pleats at the back allowed to hang loose from the neckline, the front pleats from the shoulders meeting at the waist and the gap filled in with a stomacher, and then falling loose to the hem. The bodice would be close-fitting at the sides with robings to the waist in a later version. Any style of hoop could be worn beneath these loose gowns. The sac style lost popularity in the 1780s, but could be worn as an open robe from about 1750. The open bodice was worn with a stomacher or false front, and from the 1760s, robings, now decorated or embroidered, could reach the ground. From about 1770 the bodices were closed in the front with an edge to edge fastening, and the back, beneath the loose flowing material eminating from the neckline, was still laced to give the bodice a good fit. Sleeves were close fitting to the elbows with several deep flounces. Winged or round cuffs with small frills were also seen.

The overskirt was still constructed as previously with an inverted V in front and was often worn with the corners of the front hitched up to form bunches at the rear. In the 1760s the overskirts were trained, but became shorter again later. Petticoats followed the lengths of the overskirts and

Wrapping gown, a closed robe style worn with a pannier. The sleeve cuffs are lace ruffled and the modesty piece is also of lace, c 1745

High-waisted gown with the skirt trained behind. The high décolletage is trimmed with lace. The cap is of the pinner type decorated with flowers and frills and held on with ribbons. Suspended from the wrist is a reticule closed with a drawstring, c 1799

were decorated with flounces. A chemise style gown was very fashionable from about 1785 and was usually of a fine delicate material. The close-fitting bodice had a low round décolletage edged with a falling collar, vandyked, and often of lace.

Sleeves could be long and tight, buttoned at the wrists. The long skirts were either gathered or pleated to the bodice and could have the hems either plain or left loose.

If the gown was closed all round, it was put on over the head, but it could also be fastened with buttons or ribbon ties from bosom to hem.

Round gown

From about 1794 most dresses became high waisted and the general silhouette became more elongated as the bustle at the back and the front buffon diminished. The trained skirts became longer behind and placket holes were seen less as bags were being used instead of hidden pockets.

Those dressed in Classical styles were made of lighter materials, such as muslins, and were worn throughout the year. Décolletages became higher.

The classical style of open robe had a short bodice with a wrap-over front joined to the trained overskirt open with an inverted V in front revealing the petticoat. The collar of the bodice could be a continuous roll around the V shaped neckline. If the sleeves were long they were tight fitting, if short they were generally puffed. A low necked bodice worn over a round gown could be lace or tied. The overskirt was trained, covering only the back and was in a contrasting colour. The bodice sleeves were usually short enough to reveal the sleeves of the round gown. The bodice of the round gown was usually high necked appearing above the lower neckline of the overgown. The collar could be standing or have a small neck ruff. A round gown could also be worn with a low necked overbodice reaching the thighs. This was often short sleeved to reveal the high collar and long sleeves of the round gown itself. A ribbon belt could be worn around the waist. Another style which could be worn over a round gown and also over the overbodice made similar to a corset, was a short-sleeved, basqued bodice fastening with jewelled buckles or lacing. These varied in design and could be short or long like a half robe. They were also known as *vests* if they had no sleeves.

Morning or informal wear

An informal version of an open gown was the *trollopee* which had an unboned bodice with a trained overskirt and a short petticoat. As this was mainly an indoor garment a hoop was not always worn.

Skirts and bodices could be separate. The bodice could then be a type of jacket, tight fitting and flaring out at hip level, fastening down the front with lacing or hooks and eyes that could be concealed by a fly. If left partially open a waistcoat could also be worn. The elbow-length sleeves could have winged cuffs or laced frills. Another bodice style, known as a *pet-en-l'air*, was popular from the 1750s and was a jacket with a sac back, slightly longer than the one described above, with robings and a stomacher. The sleeves were long and tight fitting with round cuffs and ruffles.

Petticoats were often trimmed with flounces, and were mainly worn over domed hoops or panniers.

In the 1780s a *caraco*, a close fitting thigh-length jacket flared from the waist without a waist seam, but often had a waist sash or girdle. The *juste*, similar to the caraco, had a waist seam from which the skirts flared. These could be longer at the back or might be tabbed. The low décolletage ended with a falling collar and the bodice itself closed in the front with hooks or lacing over a stomacher. The base of the petticoats worn with these jackets was flounced and edged in matching lace.

A *nightgown* or négligée was an informal open robe with robings and stomacher. It was unboned, worn with a fill-in at the décolletage and often with a white apron.

The Italian nightgown or robe, often of Italian silk, was popular in the 1770s and more fashionable than the négligée. The bodice, without robings and tight fitting had edge to edge closure ending in a point at the front. The back had whalebone stiffeners inserted in the seams. The long sleeves were cuffed. The overskirt joined to the bodice in pleats was left open in front and the trained back hitched up. There were several methods of hitching up – points could be fastened with a button and loop at hip level or drawstrings were passed through loops from the hemline to waist where a tassel was attached. The petticoat was generally of a different colour with trimmings or fringing. Short aprons of flimsy material could be worn with this style.

Side view of a short polonaise. The skirt and overskirt are flounced. The short sleeves are worn with a large frill. The large lace hat worn at a forward tilt is profusely decorated with frills and flowers. A folding fan is carried in one hand, *c* 1780

Back view of a polonaise looped in three puffs, *c* 1777

Polonaise

The *polonaise* became very popular in the period between 1770 and 1790. the most fashionable versions were short. The essential feature of a polonaise was the overskirt that was hitched up into three distinct draperies behind, thus exposing the petticoat all round. Usually a central drape at the back was longer than the two side ones, although all three could be of equal length, depending on the choice of the wearer. The drapes were formed with a running cord threaded through loops up the seams and pulled up to the waist held with buttons and loops or ribbon ties with stitching separating the three puffs and bows sewn on each side of the central back puff.

The petticoats worn with the short polonaise had deep flounces or quilting around the base. They were shorter than usual, just reaching the ankles. The long polonaise, popular just briefly between 1780 and 1785 had a trained overskirt caught up in three puffs. The petticoats with this style were long, covering the ankles. The bodice was without robings and fastened in the front with an edge to edge closure with either buttons, hooks and eyes or lacing.

The décolletage could be square or round fastened at the bosom with a breast knot. If the gap was large, a blunt-pointed or tabbed waistcoat was worn. Stomacher fronts were also seen, or if the décolletage was not so large, a zone could be worn. The back of the bodice was close fitting and could continue into the flared overskirt of the polonaise. Alternatively it could be joined to the overskirt which was closely pleated to the slightly dipped back.

The sleeves could be of any length. If elbow length they were generally

Riding costume. The jacket decorated with frogging is worn open. The waistcoat buttoned in the male fashion from left over right and comes to points in the front. The beehive hat is worn over a high coiffure.

This riding habit consists of a coat, waistcoat and petticoat. A Steinkirk cravat is worn and a tricorne hat is being carried under her arm, c 1715

cuffed with perhaps some frilling. The three-quarter length sleeves were always frilled as were the long tight-fitting sleeves with wrist buttons and cuffs.

Riding costume

Riding costumes were worn for travelling in general and consisted of a jacket, waistcoat and skirt. The jacket was double-breasted with the skirts curving back to form short tails. The front skirts of the jacket were joined at the seam at the waist to flare out, giving a better fit over the full skirt. Apart from this the jackets were very similar to a man's frock coat with a back vent and the side vents with a pocket. At first they were high necked without collars, but by about 1765 small turned-down collars were present. As the jacket became more open, the collar was stepped to form lapels. Sleeves were long and tight fitting and ended with closed cuffs. The collar and cuffs were often faced in a different colour to the jacket, but matched the waistcoat. Jackets were fastened with buttons, left over right, as were the men's. A cravat or Steinkirk was worn around the neck. The waistcoat, like the men's had the back of a cheaper material, but was made with a dart each side in front to fit the figure. A false waistcoat consisting of just the front panels could be sewn into the jacket lining. Towards the end of the century the waistline of the riding jacket became higher and sashes were beginning to be worn. The long, tight sleeves had buttons at the wrists, and from the 1770s braid edging and loops and frogging became more fashionable.

By the 1780s the waistcoat skirts which had been getting shorter disappeared leaving just the front curving to a point and the lapels became so large that they overlapped those of the jacket.

The *petticoats*, as the skirts were called, were long and slightly trained.

Outdoor wear

Cloaks were the most popular outdoor attire as coats would have been impractical with the dresses of this time. Until about 1730 tent-like ground length cloaks were worn with slits in the sides for the arms to protrude. They were buttoned down the front and had flat turned down collars. Hoods, often attached, were worn with these cloaks.

After this date the cloaks became shorter, the length varying from shoulder to below the waist. When just shoulder length, *mantlets*, as they were also known, could be worn indoors as well as outdoors.

Tippets fashionable throughout were usually of fur and worn with matching muffs. They were like shoulder capes with the ends hanging down in front. Until about 1740 a scarf was a large rounded wrap falling to the waist at the back though sometimes longer in front. This gradually evolved into a *pelerine*, encircling the shoulders at the back, falling into pendants to about the knees in front. These could be crossed over the bosom, passed around the waist and tied behind. This was another style that could be worn indoors as well. From about 1780 a large scarf worn around the shoulder with a high collar and hanging ends in the front became very fashionable. The *pelisse* worn from mid-century until about 1800 was a cape gathered to a neckline and hanging down without flares, but with slits for the arms. It could have a deep, flat collar or attached hood

Corset with back lacing, *c* 1715

Silk shoe with tongue and latchets for tying, *c* 1700-1730

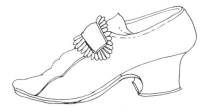

Damask shoe with a buckle, *c* 1730-50

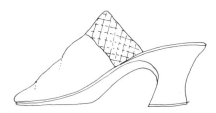

Early type of slipper, *c* 1700-1730

and was fastened in front with hooks or ties. By the end of the eighteenth century the pelisse gradually evolved into a high-waisted overcoat.

Short cloaks were also seen and worn for dress occasions, but were gored to give extra fullness. Although they might be worn open they could be fastened at the neck edge with ribbon bands.

Overcoats were first worn in the 1780s when gowns became less bulky and distended skirts were seen less often. One of the first coats was a greatcoat dress worn for riding as well as a morning walking dress, made of a thick material. The bodice was close fitting and had a double or triple falling collar and large revers. The front was always covered with a buffon or neckerchief. The skirt of the coat was ground length and full, the coat itself buttoning from the base to show the petticoat underneath. Sleeves were long and tight, buttoning at the wrists. These riding coats became known as *redingotes*. A *spencer* was a short-waisted over-jacket with long sleeves. It was shaped to the figure and had a flat roll collar.

Shawls also came into fashion gradually in the late 1700s and were often hand embroidered.

Neckwear

A square *handkerchief* or *neckerchief*, folded diagonally, was draped around the neck with the point at the back and the ends tied in a knot in front or attached to the stomacher with ribbon ties. *Kerchiefs* were usually pieces of material, but worn in the same manner.

Tuckers and *modesty pieces*, very similar to each other, were frills or ruffles, lace edged. They were attached to a low décolletage, but the modesty pieces did not continue up the sides, and only stretched across the base of the décolletage. A buffon, like a large neckerchief, was of diaphanous material. It was draped around the neck and shoulders and bunched in front, tucked into the décolletage. It could, like the neckerchief, cross over the front and tie at the back.

Ruffs were worn from the 1750s. They were quite small at first and made like a wired-up tucker, rising from the sides of the décolletage increasing in height, spreading towards the back, fan shaped. They were then known as standing frills, and worn with insets. By the 1790s ruffs became larger with double or triple circular capes to the shoulders, gathered or pleated to a neckband.

Small high ruffs were often worn as well. Small neck frills were also known as ruffs.

Cravats or *Steinkerks* were worn mainly with riding habits. These were strips of material loosely tied around the neck with the ends falling in the front. Ribbon neckbands were worn from the 1730s. These were usually black velvet and worn high around the neck, buckled at the back. In the early part of the period the ends could be worn down the front over the stomacher.

Underwear

Hoops were worn until about 1780 except for Court wear when they were fashionable until about 1820. Hoop petticoats could be of various shapes, each style having its own name. They could be dome shaped, this being achieved with seven or eight hoops in increasing width made of cane or

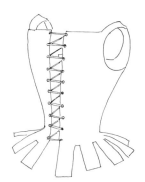

Corset with tabs at the waist,
c 1768

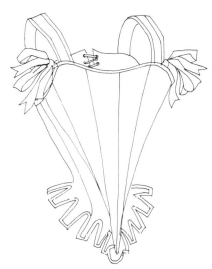

Whalebone stiffened corset with
ribbon loops, c 1715

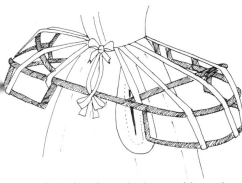

Articulated pannier hoop with a pair
of pockets beneath

whalebone and covered with a petticoat. Fan shapes came into fashion in
the 1740s and the pyramid shape was flattened front and back to give the
fan effect with the skirts curving out at the sides. Oblong hoops were very
wide from side to side, being just distended at the waist, and the skirts
allowed to hang straight down all round.

Pannier hoops were also very popular. The cane or whalebone frame
was attached each side in the form of half hoops that could be hinged so
that they could be folded if necessary. These separate cages were
attached to a waistband and tied with tapes.

Bustles also became fashionable towards the end of the eighteenth
century. These were usually made of horsehair, crescent shaped pads
fitting to the back of the waist and tied with tapes at the front. Occasionally
small hoops could be utilised instead.

At the start of the eighteenth century *corsets* were made of lavish
materials worn as bodices. They had whalebone supports, and in front
there was a hidden pocket in which fragrant herbs or sachets of perfume
could be concealed. When the Classical translucent fashions returned, a
zona was worn. This was a band of material that supported and could have
shoulder straps for support.

Footwear

Until the 1730s *shoes* were fairly pointed and had high-waisted heels. High
tongues in a variety of shapes covered the top of the shoes and were
fastened with buckles or tied over the instep. After about 1730 shoes
became daintier and less pointed and the heels not so clumsy. The tongues
also became smaller and more rounded. Small wedge heels were
introduced in the 1750s and when they were present they were placed
further forward. There were several types of heel – the Italian heels were
placed to the fore and were slender waisted, whilst the French styles,
although similar, were higher. Ornamental buckles in a great variety of
styles and designs were very popular, although occasionally rosettes or
fringed borders were also seen.

Towards the end of the eighteenth century, when pointed toes were
again fashionable, high Louis heels were worn. They took their name from
Louis XIV and were made with the sole of the shoe continuing under the
arch down the front of the heel. Ribbon rosettes as well as elaborate
embroidery replaced the buckles that had previously been so popular.
Many shoes were made in materials to match the dresses. By the end of the
century high heels and buckles again became fashionable although
buckles were being replaced by shoe laces.

About 1786 for a brief period a lower cut Chinese slipper style became
fashionable. The toes were turned up and the heels were small and low.
They were usually fastened with a running string encased in a ribbon
binding around the edge.

In the 1790s flat shoes, similar to slippers, could have small curved
wedge heels. The fronts were low and sometimes decorated with ribbon
bows. The pointed toes could curve upwards. Flat slippers resembled
modern ballet shoes, made of a soft kid and were often without any heels,
fastening in the front with ribbon bows.

Pinner with frilling and lappets, c 1785

Lunardi style hat with a puffed crown and stiff brim, c 1786

Large picture hat worn over an elaborate wig, c 1775

Half-boots with rounded toes and low heels were fastened with lacing in the front and were worn mainly for riding or driving.

With the return of the Classical styles of dress, Greek sandals with criss cross fastening up the legs were popular.

Clogs or overshoes with leather soles were worn over shoes outdoors. They were often made to match the shoes with which they were worn.

Pattens were another type of overshoe with the wooden soles raised from the ground on iron rings. The leather tops were secured to the shoes with ribbons or straps.

Stockings and tights, flesh coloured, in the Classical period, were often designed with clocks up the sides to the knees. Stockings that were worn to above the knees could be knitted in cotton or silk and in winter, of wool. They were held up with garters which were narrow lengths of material with woven-in designs and fastened either just above or below the knees.

Headwear

There was a great variety of *caps* in the eighteenth century. The fontange headdress remained in fashion until about 1714, but there were many other styles that remained fashionable throughout.

The main part of the cap was usually of a white lawn or lace with lace and other trimmings. Caps could be worn in and out of doors and could also be worn beneath hats. One style of small cap, replacing the fontange was called a *pinner*. This was small and round, worn flat on the head with a single or double row of frilling and trimmed with ribbons and lace as well as bunches of flowers. If lappets were present these could be pinned up or allowed to hang down behind. Another variation just had a little frill in the front, in a V-shaped dip, with the lappets tied beneath the chin.

Mob caps had full crowns puffed out with a frill around. Long or short side lappets were allowed to either hang down or tie under the chin. Around the caps encircling the crown was often tied a ribbon with a large bow in front.

Round-eared caps popular until the 1760s were bonnet shaped curving towards the ears with the front edged in lace. The back was usually plain, tightened with a running string to fit the head. Hair was often visible at the back with this style. Another cap, similar to the round-eared style of coif, was the *Pultney cap*, also popular from the 1760s, especially amongst the older generation, but had two wings which stood in two crescent shapes over the forehead with a centre dip in the front. Lappets, although now becoming less popular, could be present. By the 1770s when hair styles became extremely high, caps worn informally were made large enough to fit over these coiffures. The crowns were large and trimmed with ribbons, bows and lace frills. Worn formally the caps were quite small and worn perched high on top.

Butterfly caps, mainly for Court wear, were of lace wired in the shape of a butterfly, made of lace and ornamented with jewels and flowers and worn perched forward.

Hoods remained popular headwear until the 1760s, often attached to cloaks. They were large enough to cover both hair and caps and were always unstiffened. They were made of varous materials such as velvets

Patten decorated with silk damask,
c 1730-50

Shoe worn with a clog, c 1740

Mob cap, c 1780

Bergère style with a small crown
and large brim, c 1750

Round eared cap, c 1745

and satins or quilted materials. Those of a finer material and made separate to cloaks were often lace trimmed. The backs of the hoods were gathered or pleated and sometimes had side lappets tied either under the chin or crossed and fastened behind.

Hoods were attached to shoulder capes; an example of this is the capuchin or riding hood faced in a coloured lining. Hoods were less popular after the 1770s except for riding, when the *calash* made its appearance. This was a tall construction of cane or wire made to fold back when not in use.

It was usually covered in silk and the front edge trimmed with lace frills, tying in the front with a bow under the chin. As the industry for making plaited straw expanded, hats made of that material gained in popularity. A fine wheat straw imported from Italy was used for making the well-known leghorn and chip, which was willow or poplar, an alternative straw used in hat making. Many shallow-crowned hats were made of straw; perhaps one of the most popular was the bergère or shepherdess style. This was low-crowned with a wide brim and tied under the chin with ribbon bows which passed from the crown over or under the brim.

Day caps were generally worn under hats except when riding. When the hairstyles of the 1770s became elaborately high, hats varied from being small and perched on top, to enormous sizes designed to accommodate the high headdresses. The large hats were profusely ornamented with ribbon bows. By the 1780s when most hats were large, they could be worn at all angles. One such style was the picture hat with a small crown and large brim ornamented with feathers and ribbons. It could be worn tilted back or sideways.

Tall-crowned hats known as *bonnets* were generally flat topped with a small brim which could be lace trimmed. Feathers and bows or flowers often decorated the crowns, and veils were also seen in varying length.

Large soft hats with the crowns puffed and made of silk or gauze supported inside with a stiff lining were known as *lunardi* or balloon hats. Until the hairstyles became too high *jockey caps* were worn for riding. These were round crowned with a peak in front. A type of *bicorne* with the brim turned up and fastened to the crown with a rosette, loop or cockade become fashionable.

In the 1780s a hard, low-crowned round hat similar to a bowler hat with a rolled up brim and decorative hatband was worn, usually at a slightly forward angle.

Hairstyles

The eighteenth century began with simple low hairstyles. Wigs and false hair became less fashionable, being worn mainly for Court occasions, or riding. Simple hairstyles included hair being combed back and allowed to fall in loose waves or curls or a bun worn at the back of the head.

Particularly popular for fashionable occasions was a style in which the hair was allowed to fall in ringlets from a centre parting with pearls or ribbon knots entwined in it. Another favourite style, known as *tête de mouton*, had the hair styled in close curls with false curls sometimes added, decorated with topknots or artificial flowers.

In the 1760s hairstyles again became more elaborate and false

Tête de mouton hairstyle with curls and a bow and feather decoration, *c 1745*

hairpieces were added. The hair was worn high with rows of horizontal curls and feather ornamentation.

By the 1770s hairstyles had reached enormous heights with equally fantastic hair ornamentations. Padded foundations or wire supports gave extra height. The hair at the back was in a chignon, plaited or twisted and looped up. The front usually an elaboration of curls, with several allowed to hang down. These hairstyles were fixed with pomade and powdered and were left untouched for weeks. The elaborate ornamentations which included miniature gardens and model ships were however removed at night. As the hairstyles became more and more ornate and elaborate ladies resorted to wigs again, which could be removed at night. The hairstyles reached a height of 90 cm (36 in.) by the 1780s, after which date they began to diminish in height, but increase in width, and the hair frizzed to the sides covering the ears. This became known as the *herrison* or *hedgehog style*. For riding a popular hairstyle was the long hair at the back turned up into a loop and tied, like a chignon with a large bow.

Cap with short lappets worn on top of an extremely high hairstyle, *c 1776*

Hedgehog hairstyle with the hair frizzed and curled, *c 1775*

Large mob cap with a bow decoration, *c 1788*

Ribbon and feather decorated tall hairstyle, *c 1782*

Long hair worn in ringlets, *c* 1789

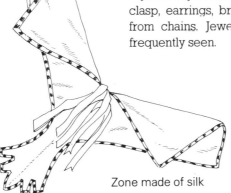

Hair worn long and loose over the shoulders, *c* 1791

Beauty aids and accessories

White lead was still used in cosmetics although it was known to be harmful to the skin. Face patches used to hide blemishes were still worn, as were plumpers to fill out the hollows of cheeks by the loss of teeth.

Perfumes and lavender waters were used in abundance, and perfumed sachets were often sewn inside the linings of garments.

Aprons in varying lengths continued to be worn. They were gathered at the waist and tied at the back with running strings.

Washable, *detachable sleeves* for informal day wear were worn from wrist to elbow, often over more ornate sleeves.

Elbow length *gloves* in a variety of materials were worn mainly on dress occasions whilst short ones were worn for riding and short sleeved dress. Mittens were usually elbow length with a separate open thumb. The back of the mittens were often embroidered and the tops could be folded down to form a cuff.

Muffs became smaller after about 1710, but by the 1780s they again became larger and were worn for many occasions. They could be of fur and often decorated with embroidery or ribbons and flowers.

Until the Classical look with its more clinging silhouette became fashionable *pockets* were a separate item, made in pairs joined by a band worn beneath a gown and accessible through placket holes or slits in the sides.

Reticules or knotting bags made in varous shapes and drawn together at the top with a running string became very fashionable. They were carried suspended from the wrist.

Fans became more popular as the century progressed. Very fashionable were the folding ones.

Masks lost their popularity about 1760.

Jewellery consisted mainly of pearl necklaces fastened with a diamond clasp, earrings, bracelets, lockets, pendants and miniatures suspended from chains. Jewelled buckles on girdles as well as footwear were frequently seen.

Zone made of silk

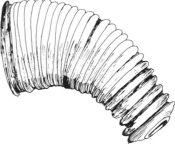

Powder puffer for hair and wigs, *c* 1770

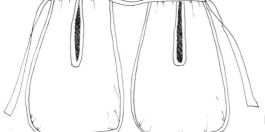

Pair of pockets, *c* 1774

Back view of an Empire line dress with short puffed sleeves and a neck ruff and elbow length sleeves, *c* 1806

High-waisted Empire style dress worn with a frilled lace cape. The mittens reached above the elbows and the bonnet-like hat is held on with a ribbon bow, *c* 1806

Nineteenth century

In the early years of the nineteenth century the simple Classical trends of previous years continued. The higher waistlines, first seen towards the end of the eighteenth century, were at their highest about 1805. The Greek Classical influence was very apparent as women dampened their flimsy muslin draperies so that they clung to the figure. The semi-transparent materials used for the dresses revealed the pantaloons worn beneath. Day and evening wear was very similar, the exception being that for evening attire the dresses were more ornate.

Daywear

The Classical styles or, as they were also known, *The Empire Line*, was often trained with low décolletages and either long or short sleeves. The ornamentation was Egyptian, Etruscan and even Gothic. These fashions were suited particularly to the younger generation as their charm depended much on the physique of the wearer. The Victorian Gothic styles, on the other hand, was more adaptable to all ages, concealing physical imperfections and adding dignity to the matron. The back seam of the bodices were set far back, giving the impression of a very small back. Sleeves were also set far in. Bodice fronts could be gathered at the waistline and the décolletage, if low, filled in with a *fichu*. Another variation was crossed over in front or gathered in at the neckline with a drawstring. An Empire gown style had just such a gathered neckline with a trained skirt that could be looped up by a cord and suspended from the back of the shoulders. If the neckline was high a small neck ruff could be worn. Another style had a low décolletage with a skirt that was straight in front and slightly gathered at the hips and back to allow for free movement. Sometimes the side seams were slit. Occasionally an overtunic was worn.

The *Greek style* was almost always trained slightly at the back. A garment with the bodice and skirt in one was usually fastened at the back and was untrained. The neckline being edged with a small frill or ruff, low décolletages were filled in with *chemisettes* or *tuckers*.

Until about 1810 dresses were worn with a fall in the front of the skirt. The upper part of the skirt was open at the side seams forming pocket placket holes with the top of the flap gathered on a running string and tied at the back of the waist like an apron. The bodice was wrapped or crossed over like a shawl, or was of a *cottage* front style, the front of the bodice laced

Morning dress with a close-fitting waist and a flounced skirt. The bodice had V-shaped ornamentation from the shoulders to the waist and the long sleeves have similar decoration, c 1842

The high-necked dress has puffed undersleeves. A poke bonnet and short gloves are also worn, c 1850

together showing a habit shirt underneath. Another style was a waistcoat bosom, by which the bodice buttoned down the front. Chemise robes fastened down the front with buttoning to the hemline. Skirts were slightly gored to give fullness without bulk. The waistline was slightly lowered when the Gothic superceded the Classical styles, and the waistline was lowered to the more natural position.

From the 1820s the shoulder line widened and puffed sleeves gave a broader appearance, balancing the fuller skirts which ended just above the ground. The wide gigot sleeves were puffed at the shoulders in many cases with ornate epaulettes or short oversleeves known as *mancherons*. The fullness was held tight to the wrists with ruffles, whilst another style – the *demi-gigot* – became tighter from the elbows. These styles were also known as *leg-o'-mutton* sleeves. An *imbecile* sleeve, full to the wrists was gathered to a close-fitting cuff. Fullness was generally achieved with either padding or stiff lining. Waistlines became lower facilitating the tight lacing.

By the 1830s the whole silhouette had changed, the large gigot sleeves disappeared and the typical Victorian look of prim sentimentality replaced the Romantic, Classical styles.

From hem to knee level skirts were often decorated with a profusion of trimmings. As the skirts became wider at the base, the hems were padded to weight down the skirts and was also used as a form of decoration. Between the later 1820s and 1830s the high necked bodices had small turned down collars or a collar that spread over the shoulder like a cape.

The bodice ended with a point and was pleated from the shoulders down. V-shaped fichu robings or lapels converged from the shoulders to waist, helping to give the impression of a small waistline. Belts or sashes were also worn. In 1836 the wide shoulders and sleeves, small waists and full skirts became softer in shape, the sleeves becoming smaller, sloping over the shoulders. The sleeves were still full, but were not stiffened and were allowed to fall loose to the wrists where they were gathered on to a closed cuff. These were similar to bishop sleeves. Another style, *en bouffant*, was puffed, with tight bands at intervals down the arm. After 1836 skirts again became longer, reaching almost to the ground. They were gathered or pleated at the waist with placket openings for access to the pockets that were tied around the waist beneath the skirt.

The characteristics of the 1840s were drooping shoulder lines with tighter sleeves, well-fitting bodices ending at a tightly corseted waist with almost gound length full skirts. By the 1850s the climax of early Victorian dress was a skirt so domed and full that it had to be supported by a hooped cage with up to six petticoats beneath. Bodices and skirts were often separate.

Towards the later years of the 1860s the fullness of the skirts was pushed towards the back, leaving the front flatter, thus reviving the bustle. If skirts and bodices were separate they could be of different colours. Necklines varied in shape. High necks decorated with braids to give a square or yoked effect. It was also fashionable from about 1866 to have ribbons and streamers trailing behind from the neckline.

Bodices were usually straight at the waist, a belt or sash being tied in a large bow.

In the 1840s day dresses with the bodice and skirt in one were trimmed

Promenade dress in a polonaise style. The bodice coat buttons down the front, and the back of the skirt is puffed out, c 1883

Bolero jacketed costume with large sleeves, c 1895

from shoulder to waist in a point front and back. The bodice was also draped across the front forming a V-shaped décolletage. The skirt was *en tablier*, with a false front, or flounced.

The *Princess* style first appeared around 1848 and was without a waist seam, the bodice and skirt cut in one in gores. The back and sides were peated to give extra fullness, an the skirt often trained.

Double skirts were fashionable, the upper skirt cut in the Princess style with the back slightly longer than the front to reveal the underskirt. In the 1870s the Princess polonaise was very popular, the long trained overskirt behind was draped and the sides looped up. The front was closed with buttons to the waist revealing the underskirt.

Another popular style in the 1870s was the *Dolly Varden*, similar to the polonaise except that the front overskirt was shorter and the back and sides were bunched up.

About 1879 Lily Langtry popularised a knitted jersey material dress that was close fitting to about mid thigh with a broad belt around the knees, the lower part was often pleated.

By the 1880s most dresses, apart from those made on the Princess cut, were separate bodices and skirts, but a high waisted style remained popular until the end of the century, this was known as the *Empire line*. The high waisted effect was achieved with a wide sash and was made fashionable by the actress Sarah Bernhardt, about 1883.

A *jacket bodice*, fashionable from about 1846, was close fitting, fastening down the front with basques or short skirts at waist level. The *caraco*, usually thigh length, was a kind of jacket with basques, the fronts being curved with rounded corners and usually only fastened to the waist. The neck opening could be V-shaped with revers or small collar. By the 1860s the jackets had a waist seam that joined the bodice to the basques.

In the 1860s the forerunner of blouses, the *Garibaldi*, was a shirt worn tucked into a skirt, in contrast to bodices that were worn separately but on the outside, usually long waisted and ending in a point in the front. Bodices were darted each side of the waist, lined and boned. The Garibaldi shirts were usually red with black braid and buttons. The high collar was narrow with points in the front. The sleeves were fairly full and gathered at the wrists. These blouses were usually worn with full black skirts which had a matching red band around the hem, and a braided bolero.

About 1874 a *cuirass* bodice became very popular. This was tight fitting like a corset, continuing over the hips, often ending in a point in the front, with a *plastron* front of a material in another colour. This matched the *tablier* of the skirt. The plastron front simulated a blouse or waistband; its three-quarter length sleeves were tight fitting. By about 1881 the bodice was ususally pouched. In the 1880s a *coat bodice* was close fitting with either basques or short tails; it had hip buttons and closed down the front with buttoning from a high neckline or a V-shaped neckline with revers. It was often worn with a pleated high necked habit shirt front. By the 1890s bodices gave a very wide appearance with a frilling forming a V from the shoulders to the centre at the waist. Lace yokes were often seen and bolero or *zouave jackets* were also popular. About 1887 blouses were loose, drawn in at the waist with a belt, or box pleated. The loose styles had shoulder yokes on to which the blouse was gathered. Collars were small

Mantle decorated with beaver fur,
c 1885

Dress with matching bolero jacket
and gigot sleeves, c 1897

and lace frilling down the front was not uncommon. From about 1877 *Norfolk jacket* styles ending at the hips became popular. These were similar to male styles, box pleated on to a yoke and were usually worn with trained pleated skirts, or in the 1890s, with plainer ones. *Gilets* were often worn, left open. They could also be made in one with the bodice, just the front simulating a waistcoat.

Sleeves were tight fitting with oversleeves or *mancherons* at the shoulders. Long sleeves, puffed to the elbow and then tight to the wrist, were worn from the 1840s. Bell shaped sleeves tight to the elbows and then opening out were worn from about 1845. In the 1850s *pagoda* sleeves expanding from the shoulders and often longer at the back were replaced by another style, the *bishop* sleeve, which was full and pleated at the shoulders, and gathered on a band at the wrist. By the late 1850s many sleeves began to be made with outer and inner seams, slightly shaped at the elbows. When sleeves became fuller at the shoulders they became known as *peg topped* and from about 1885 the tops were cut so full as to give a kick-up effect. By 1895 these gigot sleeves developed to enormous dimensions, but by 1897 they again became smaller, until by the end of the 1890s they were again quite smooth.

Long full skirts just cleared the ground in the 1840s and were lined except for summer wear. They were gathered at the waist with most of the fullness at the back. The numerous petticoats worn beneath gave a domed effect and the flounces that at first were only seen at the base gradually increased towards the waist.

Many skirts were *en tablier*, trimmed in front giving an apron effect with ribbon bows that continued on the bodice.

From about 1860 gored skirts with the fullness to the back were popular. These gave a flatter appearance at the front. Towards the end of the 1860s pannier skirts with side puffs were seen.

By the end of the 1870s skirts were much less full with a train and slight bustle effect behind.

Evening and formal wear

In the early part of the nineteenth century evening gowns had trained skirts open in front revealing the lavishly ornamented petticoats. Long sleeves reached just over the hands, but short sleeves, or short oversleeves, were also seen. Tunic dresses were also popular. The tunic hung loosely from the shoulders or tied with a sash at the waist. It was worn over long dresses in the first few years of the century. By the 1830s a tunic, of a diaphonous material, was often worn with one side looped up and decorated with either ribbon loops or artificial flowers.

The dresses were made in similar styles to those worn for day wear, except that the décolletages were low, often heart shaped. They could be decorated with lace and ribbon bows down the front.

Sleeves were at first short and puffed, but by about 1829 became larger and distended with whalebone hoops. Long transparent oversleeves were also worn. Ribbon knot decoration was seen on the shoulders and sleeves. In the 1840s many evening dresses were off-the-shoulder, with the décolletage either heart shaped or straight across. The boned bodice

High-waisted ball gown with a low décolletage, *c* 1804

Evening wear, high waisted with trained skirt. The headwear is close fitting with high feather decorations, *c* 1805

Evening gown with the pointed bodice draped. The trained skirt is flat in front and the base and shoulder straps of fur, *c* 1894

Ankle-length ball gown with a small waist and sloping shoulders with wide puffed sleeves, *c* 1830

Teagown. The bodice fastened on the left, and the long tight sleeves have double shoulder capes, *c* 1897

Riding costume profusely decorated with braid and frogging. The tall hard hat is decorated with feather and plumes, c 1818

A masculine style riding habit with a hitched-up skirt. The hard tall hat is trimmed with a broad scarf, c 1888

often came to a point at the waist, a deep *bertha* of lace covering the arms and shoulders.

By the 1850s a V shaped neckline was also popular with a false stomacher. There was always a great deal of decoration such as artificial flowers, ribbons or lace. The sleeves were often puffed and ended just above the elbows.

In the 1860s the Princess cut was also worn for evening dress with low décolletages. Separate bodice and skirt were also worn. The bodices were very low cut, even off-the-shoulder, and from about 1865 shoulder straps or ribbon bows often replaced sleeves. The long, trained skirts were greatly ornamented and looped up to reveal a petticoat trimmed with puffs. *Peplums* were also worn.

From about 1887 the drapery was being replaced by pleats as well as pleated flounces or frills at the base of the skirts.

The general trend of evening dress was to follow those worn in the daytime, but with more ornamentation and lower necklines. By about 1895 the backs also had low décolletages and as the large puffed sleeves were so low on the shoulders the straps had to be added to give extra support to the bodice.

For Court wear hooped petticoats were essential until 1820. These were then replaced by trained robes draped over embroidered petticoats. High ostrich headdresses as well as tiaras were very fashionable. Long, white kid gloves were a necessary accessory.

Wedding dresses

The styles of wedding dresses were very similar to day dresses, but they were of a white satin or silk with lace decoration overlays and a white pelisse with swansdown trimmings. The bodices were usually high necked, but if low, were always filled in with a chemisette. Veils usually covered the face. Orange blossom wreaths were also worn.

Mourning costume

Black was the usual colour for mourning although dark brown was occasionally seen. Jet trimmings and black crêpe decorated dresses and coats alike. Black veils were worn over headwear and gloves and even handkerchiefs were black, although in half-mourning a little white was seen.

Informal and sports wear

A dress specially designed for walking appeared at the beginning of the century. This was untrained and the hem was edged with small tucks, later flounced or scalloped, ending just above the ground. The sleeves could be in a different colour. These dresses were also worn for tennis until about 1888 when blouses and skirts became fashionable. Black canvas shoes, jockey caps and gloves were also worn with tennis outfits.

Tailor-made costumes became fashionable from about 1878 allowing more freedom of movement. They were first worn for sport and informal occasions. Tailored costumes with plain shirt blouses became very

Short jacket worn with a frill-fronted blouse and bloomers. A veil is worn over the low crowned boater hat, *c* 1894

Bathing costume consisting of a long short-sleeved tunic tied with a sash at the waist, worn over ankle-length drawers, *c* 1881

fashionable when by the 1890s English tailor-mades had become firm favourite for morning wear. Blouse bodices became more ornate.

Dresses worn for riding had bodices with short basques. The bodice could be double breasted with a collar. It was often left open to reveal the habit shirt beneath. Sometimes the bodice was joined to the skirt at the back only, but very often skirt and bodice were separate. The long sleeves ended with cuffs and followed the prevailing fashions. By the 1830s the bodice could be buttoned down the front and have a failling or small turned down collar and lapels. Collar and cuffs could be lace trimmed. The long skirts were sometimes trained, with pantaloons worn beneath. Black beaver hats with feather decoration and half-boots were worn for riding, as were tan leather gloves.

In the late 1800s ladies wore *Norfolk jackets* and shorter skirts under which they wore knickerbockers for shooting.

In the 1800s short jacket bodices or Norfolk jackets and box pleated skirts were worn for cycling, but knickerbockers and bloomers were found to be more practical. *Trousers*, or divided skirts, as they became known, finally became popular for cycling. Very often a cape skirt, which was a cape but could be fastened around the waist to hide the trousers was often also worn. Jockey caps or bowler hats were also worn.

Bloomers or trousers quickly became popular for other pastimes when the long skirts were too awkward.

From the mid 1800s *bathing costumes* were made in one with the bodice being high necked with a sailor collar. The trouser part often had a short overskirt added. By the 1880s bathing outfits could be made in two, a long tunic with short sleeves worn over drawers gathered in at the ankles, but by the 1890s the tunics became shorter with a belt around the waist and were worn over shorter trouser and bodice ensembles.

For informal occasions a form of négligée or morning dress was worn, open in front revealing the underdress. The sleeves were generally long and the pelisse robe style often had revers.

Teagowns were very popular from the late 1870s. They were fairly loose and worn without corsets, mainly in the afternoons when ladies relaxed before changing into the more formal evening attire. They were made in various styles with a sac back and trained to a Princess line. By about 1883 teagowns were also made in a high waisted fashion. There was usually a profusion of trimmings and lace on the sleeves, neckline, hem and front of the gowns.

Outdoor wear

A *pelisse* also known as a *carriage dress* was open down the front with a high standing collar or two or three cape collars. The back could be without a waist seam, but pleated to fit. The long sleeves were made to fit over those of the dresses, and epaulettes often decorated the shoulder seams. A sleeveless version was more like a mantle with armholes. It could be ornamented to match the dress with which it was worn and the base could be padded.

Cloaks and *mantles* were either full or three-quarter length. They were very varied and often had hoods attached. They fitted to the waist,

PLATE 3   Left *The blouse has a small high standing lace collar and is worn with a long gored skirt. The jacket has elbow-length sleeves and a caped decoration. The gloves reach the elbows. The elegant parasol is lace covered, c 1903.* Background *An open robe is worn over a petticoat and the spencer has long sleeves and small epaulettes. The brimmed hat is ornamented with plumes and worn over a lace cap, c 1819.*   Centre *Walking dress profusely decorated with pleated lace. The V-shaped neckline of the basqued jacket has velvet revers and cuffs. The jabot in front is of lace and ribbon loops. The straw hat is trimmed with flowers and feather plumes. The umbrella with a crooked handle is trimmed with pleated lace, c 1884.*   Right *The pelerine jacket sleeves are open from the elbows revealing the undersleeves or engageantes that match the decorative cap. The wide skirt is worn over a hooped petticoat, c 1857*

PLATE 4   Left *The skirt is long and straight. Button and loop decoration is seen down the side of the bodice and skirt as well as on the short sleeves. The long-handled lace frilled parasol matches the dress, c 1912.*   Background *Afternoon dress with sleeves full at the shoulders, diminishing at the elbows and ending with cuffs. The separate collar is in a plain material, the dress being in a popular spotted design. The long skirt is about 12 in. (30 cm) above the ground, c 1932.* Centre *The close fitting cloche hat has cut felt motifs either side. The popular fox fur with head, paws and tail is worn around the shoulders. The pearl necklace was fashionable and gold slave bangles are worn around the arms, c 1927.*   Right *The three-quarter length coat of the costume is single-breasted with a button link fastening. The jacket and skirt panels match the design on the jacket collar. Over the short bobbed hair is worn a large-brimmed straw hat with a deep ribbon band, c 1920*

Teagown worn with a cape collar edged in lace, c 1896

Walking dress with a spencer and pelerine, a small cape-like collar. The poke bonnet is decorated with chiffon puffs and flowers. The lady is carrying a reticule and parasol, c 1825

becoming voluminous to cover the skirts of the robes beneath. Others hung from the shoulders and had slits for the arms or loose sleeves. In the 1860s cloaks were generally three-quarter length, slightly shaped to the waist with pagoda sleeves. Collars were also seen on cloaks and mantles. A *Balmoral mantle*, similar to an *Inverness cape* had the fronts sewn into the side seams of a loose fitting coat.

In the 1880s when dress sleeves were excessive, mantles, cloaks and capes were the most practical outdoor attire, fitting at the shoulders with darts. Mantles could be caped and have large bishop sleeves. Large wired collars that stood away were also popular.

Shawls were made in a variety of ways. A *mantlet* or half-shawl was shaped to the neck with the points rounded. A hood or cape could be added. At the start of the century shawls were not very large, but were increased in size in the 1830s. Patterned and paisley designs were very popular, as was fringing. Fur *tippets* or short shoulder capes were worn in the winter.

A short jacket or *spencer* worn over a bodice was made similar to a pelisse fitted tight to the waist. It fastened down the front and the neckline could be high or V shaped. Sleeves were long for day wear, but for evenings the spencer was sleeveless.

Short loose *zuave jackets* had square fronts and military-type braid decorations. Sealskin and beaver jackets first appeared in the 1870s. Loose double-breasted jackets or *reefers* had coat-type sleeves and could be made of the same materials as the dresses, thus completing an outfit. Jackets in the 1890s could be close fitting or loose at the back with wide revers.

Pardessus or *paletots* were the names given to outdoor garments with sleeves. For evening wear they were often bell sleeved and loose fitting, but for daywear they were often tailor made, based on men's styles. From the 1850s a pelisse was three-quarter length, waisted and with bell sleeves. From about 1876 paletots made in Princess styles were a little shorter than dresses. They were slightly trained when worn over trained skirts. The turned-down collars, and lapels could be fur trimmed. Single or double breasted, fastening was with buttons down to the hem, although paletots were usually left open from the waist down.

Many other coats such as *Ulsters* and waterproof coats had a half-belt behind and even a vent, and were often tailor made. Hoods or capes could be attached. Another caped style was the Inverness coat.

Ground length *Chesterfield coats* were first seen around 1878. They were a fitted style, usually single-breasted with turned down collars and lapels that were often faced in velvet.

During the period of bustles and wide skirts, fitted coats were made to accommodate these fashions and *Dolman style* caped sleeves were worn. Three-quarter length coats were worn throughout the 1890s, single- or double-breasted. The backs were either fitted or sack backed. Covert coats were very popular worn with tailor-made costumes.

Fur coats became fashionable in the 1890s.

Walking costume trimmed with fur, matching the muff held in one hand, c 1896

The long coat has a fur collar and trimming down the front and hem. The large muff is matching, c 1827

Winter coat with demi-gigot sleeves. The low crowned hat is decorated with feathers, c 1872

Day dress worn with a matching coat, c 1879

A carriage cloak with fringing, worn over a trained dress, c 1877

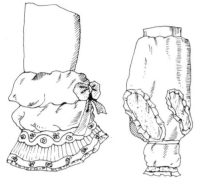

Sleeveless chemisette, *c* 1852

Detachable sleeves for a chemisette, *c* 1850

Dress accessories and neckwear

There were several types of fill-ins for low décolletages. A habit shirt or *chemisette* was made in two parts joined at the waist with tapes. The front of back could be buttoned. Sometimes the chemisette could have sleeves. These then replaced the half sleeves worn beneath pagoda or bell shaped sleeves. Informally they usually ended with cuffs, but for evening wear frilling was fashionable. Layers of lace shaped to the neckline, known as a *tucker*, were just a false front. Neckerchiefs were also worn as fill-ins. They were generally for daywear only and tied loosely in the front.

Lace *cravats* were sometimes worn with ruffs until these became unfashionable about 1836. Turned down collars became broader and a pelerine (a cape-like flat collar) or a *fichu-pelerine* was worn from about 1826. These covered the shoulders as well as the large sleeves and could be double caped, the ends of the fichu allowed to hang down the front, caught in the belt at the waist.

Separate turned-down collars with lace edging were worn with high necked bodices, and from the 1830s jackets or frilled cravats could decorate the fronts of blouses or bodices. Lace trimmed fichus crossing over in front and tied behind as well as berthas were also fashionable.

Lace tippets with long streamers were worn in the daytime, and for evening wear they were very often of swansdown.

A separate high-necked collar in tiers of lace, *c* 1807

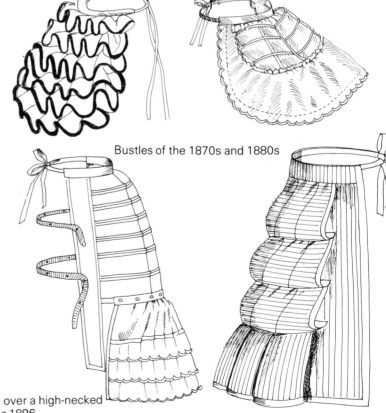

Bustles of the 1870s and 1880s

Blouse worn over a high-necked chemisette, *c* 1896

Knee length drawers. 1860s

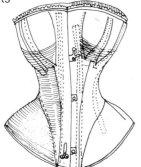

Late nineteenth century Victorian corsets

Underwear

Whilst the Classical style of dress in diaphanous materials was fashionable, underwear was sparse. The only type of corset worn was a Greek style *zona*, a kind of brassière made of silk or damask and wrapped around the upper part of the body supporting the breasts. Shoulder straps could be added. When crinolines became fashionable they were attached to tight laced corsets, the tops of which were similar to modern brassières with separate cups and the lower part reaching the top of the legs – the forerunner of suspender belts. *Drawers* for women made their appearance in the early 1800s. At first the cut was similar to the men's, each leg separately attached to the waistband. When the flimsy transparent Regency dress was the mode, they became less popular, but by the mid-century cotton or calico long drawers gathered on to a waistband tied with tapes, with an opening at the back, were in vogue. They often reached below the knees and had *broderie anglaise* trimmings. A German, Dr Jaeger, introduced natural wool for undergarments in the 1800s, this was at first considered very daring.

Pantalettes, similar to drawers, were long and straight legged reaching to below calf length; they were lace trimmed. The tops were baggy and tied at the waist. They were popular early in the century and were also called *pantaloons*. In 1851 Miss Amelia Bloomer designed a type of frilled trouser, known as *bloomers*. These were at first designed to be worn for cycling as more practical attire, but they ended as underwear.

To give the effect of the Grecian bend in the early 1800s a bustle made in a crescent-shaped roll was tied high at the back beneath the skirts.

From the 1840s to 1860s crinolines or bustles were much worn. Horsehair and crin was first used, but later whalebone, steel or cane hoops suspended by tapes were used. *Crinolettes* or half crinolines were worn when the emphasis was to the back. These were all usually worn with several layers of petticoats. Bustles in the 1880s stood out sharply at the back like a shelf. The effect was enhanced by drawing the dress back tightly over the hips and stomach, giving the appearance of a snail carrying its shell behind. These styles were worn on all occasions including sports such as tennis and skating.

Crinolines were so stiff that they could reveal the legs when moving, so long pantaloons were worn beneath.

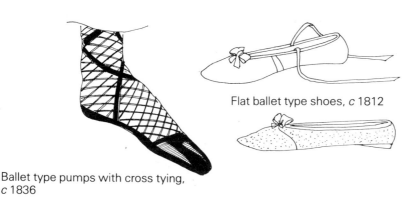

Ballet type pumps with cross tying, *c* 1836

Flat ballet type shoes, *c* 1812

Footwear and legwear

The fashion for Classical styles revived the Greek and Roman *sandals* with criss-cross lacing. Some sandals had wedge heels.

Shoes remained dainty and were often made in matching dress materials. They were generally decorated in various ways. Intricate stitched designs on the uppers, or beading and embroidery were not unusual. In the Romantic era after the 1830s shoes could be in cut designs rather like sandals with two or three bows at the instep. Heels also became higher. By the 1840s heels were lower except for boots, but by the 1850s these also became lower. As dresses became shorter and feet were visible, shoes had more decoration such as rosettes or jewellery trimmings.

By the 1880s front lacing and patent leather toecaps were seen. Lace-up walking shoes, or *Oxfords*, were made to be more practical. High fronted, and fastening with buckles, was a style known as Cromwell.

For formal occasions satin or kid slippers were fashionable and rosettes were a popular form of decoration. By about 1847 short boots could be worn for evening wear. They were often of white satin with black toecaps and decorated with jewels. Flat ballet type shoes were also worn. These had very waisted soles and hardly any heels.

House and evening *slippers*, often home made, were in delicate fabrics and were ornamented with jewelled buckles or buttons as well as rosettes.

Flat heeled shoes were also worn as slippers and until about 1807 had pointed toes, after which date they became more rounded. The toecaps were sometimes slashed to reveal the coloured linings – a short lived revival of Tudor designs. High shoes, also known as *half boots*, reached the calves and were laced or buttoned at the sides. They were generally worn for walking. They often had insoles made of plaited horsehair and covered in velvet.

By the 1830s *boots* could be worn with *gaiters*. The tops of the boots were often of cloth and in the 1870s had patent leather trimmings., Amongst the many varied styles were *Balmorals*, thick soled with lacing up the front, and perforated decoration on the sides. There were also boots with fringed tops, elastic-sided boots, high boots with tassels and heels of a different colour and many more variations.

In the early part of the nineteenth century wooden soled pattens raised off the ground with metal rings were still worn as well as leather topped clogs with cork soles in inclement weather, but later *overshoes* and *galoshes* were worn.

When semi-transparent dresses were in vogue *stockings* became more important and were mainly flesh coloured. They were often clocked or in an openwork design. They were of silk, cotton or lisle, or wool in winter. About 1815 ribbed stockings with clocks became fashionable.

Slippers and mules of the 1860s

Half boots with lacing at the side and contrasting leather trimming, *c* 1840

Elastic sided boot, *c* 1840

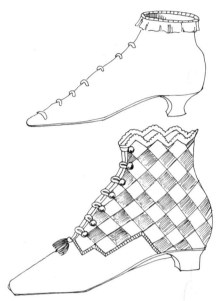

Cuffed and lace edged boots, *c* 1860

Back view of a toque decorated with feathers, *c* 1830

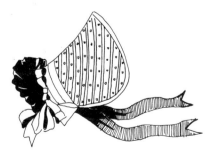

Bonnet style, *c* 1835

An innovation in the 1860s was seam and stocking knitted in one. Worn with shoes, white was a common colour, whilst with boots, stockings could be in colours and patterned. Plaid was very popular. Towards the end of the 1880s cotton and ribbed cashmere as well as plain lisle with coloured clocks were worn, but for afternoon wear silk with embroidered designs was considered more fashionable.

For balls and evening wear silk stockings were often black, although white silk openwork as well as ribbed designs were also seen.

Garters, when worn in the early 1800s, were below the knees.

Headwear

Indoor *caps* became less popular, especially amongst the younger generation, small mob caps being worn mainly beneath hats. However, formally they were still essential and were mainly in the shape of turbans. These were often made in matching fabrics, or fine materials such as net, muslin, or lamé, trimmed with feathers or lace rosettes. As hairstyles changed, turbans and caps also altered in style to accommodate the elaborate *coiffures*.

Small caps were worn towards the back of the head heavily trimmed with lace and frills forming lappets at the sides. By the 1850s caps were often triangular with ribbons hanging down the back, but by about 1855 even these were unpopular amongst the young ladies who often wore only a profusion of ribbons or lace frills in their hair, caps mainly being worn by older women. Many caps had a hole at the back to allow the hair behind to protrude. By the 1860s decorated hair nets were worn to contain the chignons.

Toques, similar to turbans or brimless hats, were worn in the early part of the century, and again became popular in the 1880s in various shapes from inverted flower pots to gable shapes trimmed with fur or feathers.

Bonnets increased in popularity from the previous century, with the crowns becoming higher around 1814 to accommodate the taller hairstyles. Poke shapes were popular with *bavolets* or frills at the back. These bavolets were fashionable from about 1828 until the 1860s. The curves of the bonnet brims increased so much in the 1820s that they had to be wired and lined. A great profusion of flowers, feathers and ribbons decorated bonnets that were tied under the chin with frills.

Soft bonnets with puffed-out crowns and stiff brims were also fashionable, and from about 1831 and oval shaped brim and very high crowned bonnet with a profusion of decorations on the underside of the brim was also very popular. This style did not need a cap underneath.

Smaller and simpler bonnets were also worn, there were fewer decorations from the 1840s, although flowers and frills were still sewn inside the brims that gradually merged with the crowns, the bonnet strings bringing the brims around the frame of the face.

By about 1853 bonnets were worn more towards the back of the head, a Mary Stuart style with a dip in the front becoming popular.

From about 1860 spoon shaped bonnets began to appear. The narrow brim at the sides rose above the forehead into a spoon shape often filled in with flowers or ribbon bows.

Low-crowned, soft-brimmed *bergere* hats, sailor styles, and flower pot

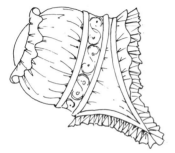

Round lace cap with lappets and tied under the chin, c 1818

Hat styles of the 1880s

Hat with a short veil, c 1870

shapes were all fashionable from the 1860s. *Glengarry caps* and *porkpie hats* were also popular as the chignon hairstyle became higher. These were usually worn tilted forward.

As hairstyles and chignons increased in popularity, bonnets became almost indistinguishable from hats, the main difference being that bonnets were tied under the chin.

Veils were often worn with bonnets to protect the face but were also worn hanging down from the back as decoration.

Until about 1875 short veils were seen on headwear, after which they became longer and could be draped around the head and neck, the ends tied in a bow in the front.

About 1883 *gable hats*, the brim pointing up sharply in front became popular. In the 1880s trimmings on headwear became excessive with the use of flowers, birds, fruit, ribbons and feathers.

Riding hats were mainly of black beaver, usually high crowned, the brims shallow or bicorne shapes. Hatbands and feathers were usual.

Hairstyles

Most new hairstyles originated in France, such as the *Titus* style with hair cut short. There were variations with the back hair hanging in ringlets as well as short curled hair. Classical Grecian and Roman style were also seen early in the century.

The Grecian fashion had the hair pulled back into curls or ringlets with false hair sometimes added to emphasise the style.

Hair was also pulled back ending in ringlets in the Roman way, the front hair curled and a bandeau worn around the head.

The *à l'Egyptienne* mode had the hair brushed back, caught in an ornamental and jewelled comb, and the hair plaited or curled. The front could be waved and rows of beads worn around the head from the forehead.

The Classical styles and short Titus hairstyles were gradually replaced by longer and softer hair fashions. Small curls were seen at the forehead and sides, and the hair at the back could be plaited into a large top knot which by the 1820s was arranged with loops and bows held up with wire frames and covered with a profusion of feathers, ribbons flowers or jewellery. Much false hair was also added. By about 1835 hairstyles again became lower with loops or knots of hair set further back, or plaits looped into a chignon. Curls or ringlets on the sides were also fashionable. Sleeker hair was seen in the 1840s, the hair lying flat from a centre parting and pulled into a chignon or bun at the back, held in place with an ivory or tortoiseshell comb. Ringlets at the sides or back, with a profusion of decoration, were fashionable as also was hair either side plaited and covered the ears.

By the 1850s the side hair was slightly puffed out and a chignon worn at the back. The chignon was fashionable, becoming fuller and held in place with a net. It could consist of masses of curls or plaits with artificial hair added. As the chignon became higher on the head, ringlets could fall down behind.

In the 1870s small fringes were seen and chignons began to decline in popularity, and if worn they were higher on the head.

Hairstyle of the 1830s

Hairstyle of the 1830s

Hairstyle of the first decade of the nineteenth century

Hairstyles of the 1870s

A new method of waving the hair with heated tongs was invented by a Parisian hairdresser, Marcel Grateau, and this become fashionable in 1870 influenced by Lily Langtry who had her hair so waved and wore a chignon low at the back. As she had blond hair this became a fashionable colour and many ladies dyed their hair.

For evening and Court wear tall ostrich plumes were a very popular hair decoration. In the 1820s when chignons were fashionable, ringlets were often allowed to fall at the back. By the mid 1800s hair was smooth in front and the sides were fluffed into soft curls or clusters of ringlets.

False hair was also used to give extra fullness. Curls were generally worn longer for evening wear. Top knots, Apollo knots and a great profusion of ribbons and flowers were used as decoration.

Beauty aids and accessories

Plumpers were still in use as the start of the nineteenth century, but this fashion died out. *Rouge* was very fashionable, but became less popular in the 1830s when the mode was to be pale and languid looking, pearl powder being used to achieve this effect.

During Queen Victoria's reign, which embraced most of the nineteenth century, make-up was regarded as improper, and it was not until Edward VII became King in 1901 that a little face powder and a modest amount of make-up was permitted.

Lavender water and cologne became more popular than the heavy perfumes in the 1850s.

Aprons were worn informally at home until the late 1880s after which they were only worn by domestic servants. At the start of the century they were usually of white muslin with small pockets, but for evening wear they were of lace and could be frilled. From about 1836 onwards aprons worn in the daytime were often bibbed, they could be embroidered or lace edged. Very small aprons were worn with teagowns.

Handkerchiefs were lace edged for evening wear whilst for daywear they had coloured borders or embroidered corners. For mourning they had black borders and designs.

It was etiquette to wear *gloves* indoors as well as out, as it was a sign of gentility. By 1830 gloves for day wear were generally short and the backs were embroidered. Evening gloves became shorter about 1836 and were often of white kid embroidered and trimmed with ruching. In the 1850s gloves became tight fitting as it was considered elegant to have small hands so they had to be buttoned at the wrists. For county wear gauntlet gloves were worn. Short mittens could also be worn in the daytime, but for evening wear they were generally longer.

Large *muffs*, fashionable at the beginning of the century, often matched *boas* and *tippets* made of fur or swansdown, but towards the 1840s muffs became much smaller.

Hairstyles of the 1870s

Handbags and reticules were still very similar to those used previously. They were often made in materials which matched the dresses with which they were used. In the 1880s clasps on bags were being used; these were made of steel or tortoiseshell.

Fans at first were fairly large, becoming smaller and were decorated with painted scenes. From the 1830s the handles could be very decorative, made of ivory, mother-of-pearl or tortoiseshell. For special occasions fans could be of ostrich feathers. By the 1870s fans again became larger.

In the 1830s *parasols* were made in pagoda shapes, as the gowns grew wider, so the parasols diminished. In the 1840s to 1860s they were at their most elegant. In the 1880s they became quite large and more dome-shaped and were often of Japanese paper. In the later 1800s when bustles were the mode, special lop-sided umbrellas were designed. The handles could be very decorative and the sticks were sometimes made telescopic. Lace or frilled edging was very popular and often parasols were made in materials to match the dresses.

The *chatelaine* in the 1840s was a development of the Elizabethan girdle, to hold small useful items such as snuff and patch boxes, keys, watches, etc.

Jewellery, as ever, was popular. By about 1810 pendant earrings became very fashionable. Short necklaces were worn in the 1830s and necklaces made of tresses of hair and velvet ribbon with a cross or heart suspended was also popular. In the 1860s dog-collar type necklaces of wide velvet decorated with jewels became modish.

Coronets and tiaras were popular for evening wear. Jet became very fashionable in Victorian times and was utilised in all kinds of jewellery as well as for buttons.

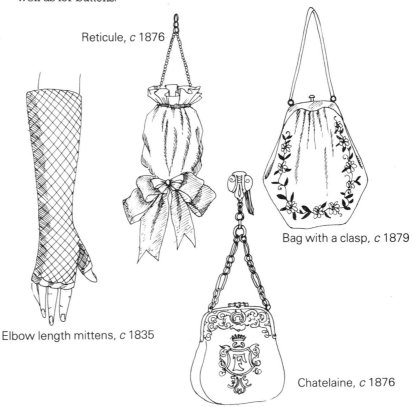

Reticule, *c* 1876

Bag with a clasp, *c* 1879

Elbow length mittens, *c* 1835

Chatelaine, *c* 1876

Gibson girl style. Shirt with cravat and long skirt and a boater straw hat, c 1900

Matching bolero and skirt worn with a high-necked blouse, c 1906

Twentieth century

A characteristic feature of the Edwardian era was a Gibson Girl style. This was an S shape achieved with a large bosom, small waist and ample posterior.

Dresses were usually in two pieces, a bodice or blouse and a skirt. Bodices were generally high necked, pouched in front. Belts were usually worn to accentuate a small waistline. The skirts were padded at the back, long at the start of the century, but by about 1915 shorter, without padding, to about 8 in. (20 cm) from the ground. By 1918 they were again calf length becoming longer in the 1920s until about 1925-1927 when they became extremely short, about 18 in. (45 cm) from the ground, the shortest that they had ever been. Waistlines dropped to about hip level about 1916.

Daywear

From as early as 1907 dresses became looser fitting and the waistline slightly raised. From about 1910 it was more general for day dresses to be in one, high collars being popular until about 1912 when V or rounded necklines became fashionable, Peter Pan or standing collars were added. The sleeves were cut in one with the bodice as well as other styles. By the 1920s dresses were plainer and skirts pleated or flared. Dresses could also be made to button down the front, usually with a belt around the waist and the collar turned down flat with revers. By the mid 1920s the neckline of dresses were of differing shapes from boat lines to V necks, worn with a scarf or fill-in, or with any number of collar styles. The bodices were plain, yoked or embroidered, with cape effects also being popular. By the end of the 1920s bodices were more bloused and the skirts draped towards one side. Dresses without sleeves of any kind could be seen in summer and for afternoon wear. By the end of the 1920s skirts were shorter than they had ever been before. It also became fashionable to have a slender boyish appearance so dresses were made straight like tubes.

The blouses of two piece dresses were often of a different material and colour to the skirt, white being very popular; jackets matching the skirts could be worn with these ensembles.

At the beginning of the century blouses with short basques were worn and until about 1906 most blouses were pouched in front. About 1909 Peter Pan collars as well as cowl necklines became fashionable. From about 1910 blouses were tucked into skirts at the waist, fastening at the back or

Straight dress worn with a cloche hat, gloves and envelope type handbag. The shoe has a bar and button fastening, *c* 1927

Blouse of the early twentieth century

Loose fitting blouse, *c* 1923

front with buttons. Blouses were made in similar styles to dress bodices. Long sleeves were generally soft and flowing, when wide they were gathered at the wrist to cuffs. Pagoda and long tight sleeves were also seen. Short sleeves were in similar styles, but ended just above the elbows.

By about 1915 skirts became fuller, either flared or bell shaped, gored or flounced. There were a great variety of styles in the 1900s. Tight at the hips and allowed to fall free at the back was a waterfall style, whilst the mermaid was tight to the knees and then flared out to give a fishtail effect. Sunray pleating and skirts with embroidered waistbands and hems were other typical modes.

Overskirts or peplums were popular, as were tunic overskirts that ended just below the knees. Hobble skirts, very narrow towards the hemline were fashionable towards 1910.

Skirt waists were often above the natural waistline, but in the 1920s they were lowered until they were below the waistline. By about 1925 when the waistline was indicated by a belt around the hips, the straighter skirts were gored. By about 1928 when the waistline was again near its natural place, skirts were at knee level again. Skirts cut on the bias often had side decorations, such as large bows, or gathered panels.

Jumpers of knitted materials such as jersey silk or wool gradually replaced blouses and shirts in popularity about 1916. They had no fastenings, being pulled over the head. They could be hip length with a belt at the waist, but by the 1930s they became shorter. Dresses made in the knitted fabric of silk or wool and without fastenings, also became fashionable.

Jumper suits consisted of skirts and matching jackets and jumpers. Two piece dresses had a skirt and matching sleeveless jacket or bolero worn with a shirt or blouse. Hems, and neck and sleeve edges of knitted clothing were very often ribbed to give a better and firmer fit and also help to keep the shape.

Two piece *tailor-made suits* originated by Charles Worth at the turn of the century and tailored skirts and coats or jackets became classic wear for town and country. They were generally worn with 'sensible' laced Oxford shoes and masculine-looking blouses with collars and cuffs. They could also have jabot fronts or scarf collars with the ends long enough to tie into a bow. These blouses were always tucked into the waistband of the costume skirt.

In the 1920s jackets were fairly straight, similar to a man's lounge suit, although basques or flounces to accentuate the hips, were seen. The lapels were pointed and the collars high. The jacket sleeves were often plain and straight with turned back cuffs.

Skirts were generally straight although they could be pleated at the side. They were often sewn on to a petersham band at the waist. Pleated or wrap-over skirts were also fashionable.

Formal suits were generally in one colour, but the more informal had skirt and jacket in different colours, with detachable sailor collars and belts or half belts at wherever the waist level was fashionable.

Trousers were first worn by women who were employed in various jobs during the First World War (1914-1918). They appeared for sport and evening wear in the 1920s.

Dress with a tabard-like overtunic,
c 1922

Hobble skirted fashion with a bolero
jacket, c 1912

Evening and formal wear

Until the first decade of the twentieth century evening dresses remained similar to the two piece day wear, but more ornate. Even the hobble skirt was worn for evening wear around 1910 with the skirt caught below the knees with a ribbon band. Overskirts were worn gathered just above the ground with a buckled sash or belt. High-waisted bodices, like a wide sash held up with shoulder straps, were in vogue.

Until the 1920s the Empire line remained fashionable. From the 1920s evening dresses tended to be tighter fitting with many dresses being backless, halter necks or straps holding the bodice up.

By about 1911 evening dresses were generally made in one piece, the bodices with low décolletages. The skirts were flared and trained with flouncing at the hem. Drapery became extremely popular as did embroidery and appliqué.

Whilst the fashion for boyish appearance persisted, evening dresses which were also straight were elaborately sequinned or beaded. However, large silk shawls often replaced evening dresses entirely. They were tightly wrapped around the body with one end thrown over the shoulders.

Overtunics with uneven hems were often seen.

For dancing the skirts were slightly shorter and much fuller with gores or sunray pleating.

For dinner wear low décolletages were often covered by transparent fill-ins; blouses and long, pleated skirts were also worn.

Court dresses, always trained, were low cut, mainly following the fashions of the day. For debutantes they were white with matching gloves and feather decoration. Long trains were pleated and attached to the gowns at the shoulders or from the waist.

Turkish style trousers, first designed by Paul Poirot, the French designer, were not popular before the war, although an outfit with trousers and top in one did become an evening fashion in the 1920s.

Pyjama suits of brocade or silk were popular as informal evening wear. For sports wear trousers had turn-ups and for beachwear were worn with blouses and boleros.

For evening wear capes with collars were still very fashionable, a popular material being velvet or silk. They could be decorated with sequins, appliqué work, ruching, embroidery or even fur. In the 1920s three-quarter length cloaks gathered at the hem to give a barrel shape were popular. The linings were also embroidered at the base as well as up the sides.

Wedding dresses, as previously, were of white satins or silks; bodice and skirt in one, following the trends of evening wear for which they could subsequently be worn. Sleeves were short and puffed or long and straight with lace oversleeves. In the 1920s wedding dresses were shorter and had uneven hemlines. Veils of a lighter lace than previously hung back forming part of a train. Orange blossom wreaths as well as Juliet caps or coronets were worn on the head. Owing to the austerity during the First World War a going-away-dress was in many cases worn in place of a white wedding dress.

For *mourning* black remained predominant, but by the 1920s the

Fashionable Charleston dance dress when they were at their shortest in 1926

Short evening dress with a cross-over bodice, c.1920

Pyjama suit worn as evening attire, c 1929

Knitted jersey jumper suit with a hip length top and pleated skirt. The close fitting hat is a turban style, c 1928

Ankle length evening dress with a small train. Long beads were very popular in the 1920s

Two-piece costume with the jacket buttoning at the waist only, c 1920

Motoring coat with the hat held down with a veil tied under the chin, *c* 1907

Knickerbocker fashion worn with a long cardigan and a beret type hat, *c* 1922

mourning period became shorter, and subdued colours such as mauve or violet, were considered fitting, with a black armband or black diamond shape sewn on to the coat sleeves.

Informal and sportswear

In the early 1900s habit jackets and apron skirts, open at the back were worn over breeches for *horse-riding*. Ankle or calf-length coats could be worn instead of jackets. If skirts were worn alone, they were divided like trousers. For *golfing* and *shooting*, skirt hems were bound with leather and were just above ground. Norfolk jackets were worn and for extra warmth knitted cardigans or pullovers were also seen, often knitted in Fair Isle patterns. Blouses and shirts were in male styles with stiff high collars and ties. When tailor-made suits became fashionable, these were also worn for sport, usually made of tweed. Coats were also worn trimmed with leather to match the skirt hems. Stiff felt hats or tweed caps were popular as well as cloche hats and later, crocheted caps. Boots and shoes were worn with gaiters and the woollen stockings were often in a checked design.

Cycling skirts were at first designed straight at the back so as not to interfere with the wheels, but by about 1911 inverted pleats at the back seemed more practical. Knickerbockers and bloomers had become unfashionable. From the early 1920s divided skirts or shorts became popular.

Tennis outfits were in white: a dress or skirt and blouse, and a straw boater. By about 1920 tennis dresses became shorter and were often cut in the Princess line. Necklines were generally V shaped with a scarf or tie worn around the collar. Instead of a hat a headband held the hair in place and eyeshades were worn against the sun. In the early 1920s the skirts were about 10 in. (25 cm) above the ground, but by about 1925 ended just below the knees, being pleated to allow far greater movement.

In the early 1900s *skating* ensembles consisted of flared skirts, hobbles when they were fashionable, although most impractical, and double-breasted coats trimmed with fur, and fur gloves, muffs and hats. By the 1920s and 1930s flared skirts became shorter and were worn with woollen pullovers and matching cloche hats.

A typical *winter sports outfit* would consist of a long woollen pullover which could be worn as a jacket with pockets, fastening with large buttons and a belt. The bottoms or trousers were tucked into thick woollen socks. Woollen gloves, scarf and peaked cap were usually made to match.

When *motoring* became more universal, the outfits at first consisted of warm clothing covered by a long, waterproof, fur-lined top coat. Warm wool veils were worn to protect the face in winter whilst for summer wear dust coats worn over summer dresses were sufficient. When hats were enormous these had to be held down with veils. Goggles were also essential to protect the eyes.

Teagowns were still made in similar styles to the late nineteenth century, but by about 1919 a pinafore style made of lightweight material became popular. During the hobble skirt period, the tight skirts were hidden by draped over-skirts, panels also being fashionable.

In the early 1920s teagowns were more like formal afternoon or semi-evening dress. They were made of delicate materials and worn over satin

Tennis outfit, c 1919

Skating costume, c 1927. The jumper, cardigan and scarf arc matching. The short skirt is pleated and the fashionable high boots have skates attached

Afternoon dress with a low décolletage and a chiffon fill-in. The hemline is uneven and over the dress is worn a matching three-quarter length coat with fur trimmings, c 1928

Walking costume with three-quarter length jacket. The collar is fur trimmed and the matching muff has three tails, c 1907

Swimming costumes (a) c 1910 (b) c 1903

The fur trimmed coat with a matching fur stole has large pockets at the hips, c 1918

The single-breasted wrap-over coat has a stand-up collar and fastened with a buckle at the waist, c 1924

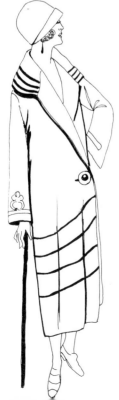

foundations or petticoats. The bodices were either crossed over or had low décolletages with jabot inserts. The sleeves ended at the elbows or were long and frilled. Sashes were often so long that they formed a train at the back. Skirts were pleated or panniered and the hems scalloped.

Outdoor wear

Capes and *cloaks* were still worn at the beginning of the century, often made of reversible tweeds. *Paletots* were also still seen with up to three attached capes. *Basqued jackets* with wide revers and high or Medici collars were still fashionable. Machine or handknitted short coats or jackets, known as sports coats, though not necessarily worn just for that purpose, were first made like fitted cardigans, but by about 1912 were loose fitting and hip length, closing with buttons or a belt at the waist. The collars were flat and wide lapels reached down the hem of the cardigan. These cardigan jackets were mainly worn over summer wear, and were also made to match skirts.

Ulster coats were popular, made in many styles, three-quarter length or long, fitted or loose. *Raglan* coats with the sleeves cut in one with the main body of the coat were also fashionable.

Many coats had decorative embroidered edges, and large buttons were very fashionable from about 1910. Single- or double-breasted styles were worn. Some coats fastened with just one button on the left and had long roll collars. For summer wear coats were in silk or satins, and lace trimmed. For the winter they were lined and fur collars and trimmings were fashionable. Fur and imitation fur was used extensively as trimming on collars, cuffs hems and even pockets. Fur coats usually had roll collars and fastened with one button to the left. They were generally lined in satin.

By about 1916 coats became shorter and were military looking, influenced by the First World War. They were still caped and had flared skirts with high, turned down collars. A military type of trench coat with deep collars with revers and large pockets and belted was copied from the officers uniform. The deep cuffs were elasticated at the wrist to keep out the wet and cold.

Coats were made in many styles and lengths with shoulder yokes or pleating from the shoulders, long or three-quarter.

About 1919 barrel shapes were fashionable with emphasis on the hips; they had large pockets.

Very large collars were the mode in the 1920s as were three-quarter length coats Looser raglan types were also popular. Wrap over coats fastened with a large button just below the waistline and sometimes had a half belt at the back.

Coats in general followed the trend of dress lengths and were sometimes made to match. The coat linings were often of the same material as the dresses with which they were worn, especially summer wear.

Underwear

The clinging gowns of the Edwardian period were worn over straight-fronted *corsets* that thrust the bosom forward and the posterior back, giving the fashionable S shape. Padding was used above and below the waist so that the waist appeared even smaller. The corset had long metal stays in the front, fastening with hooks and eyes. The *stays* were worn over

The brassière is stiffened with whalebones and has adjustable straps, *c* 1905

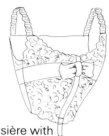

Lace decorated brassière with elastic straps, *c* 1913

Dress shield with lacing at the back, *c* 1925

Corsets with suspenders (a) *c* 1905, (b) *c* 1914

Satin girdle with suspenders, *c* 1914

a chemise which was tucked into drawers. The tops of the chemise were so tight that they supported the breasts. About 1913 *brassières* were introduced to help emphasise the required shape. In the 1920s corsets were designed to reduce the hips and when in the mid 1920s a flat shape was the mode, the corset-brassière was so designed – like a very wide bandage.

With the growing popularity of sport and more emphasis on comfort, tight laced corsets became less popular and evolved into girdles from waist to groin only. These had suspenders added and could be worn equally as suspender belts.

Drawers were mainly in white, pink or black, with wide leg openings, or a tighter fitting shorter style, the forerunner of panties and briefs.

About 1928 *camiknickers* became fashionable. These were a petticoat top with attached knickers with a flap fastening between the legs. These were superceded in the 1930s by camisole tops and loose knickers, lace frilled around the leg. *Suspender belts* also became less fashionable for a while, stockings being held up with garters above the knees. The brassière was the only close fitting undergarment which remained.

Footwear and legwear

Shoes were made in a variety of leathers, suede being one of the most popular. After the First World War crocodile and other exotic snake skins became the vogue with handbags made to match.

From about 1910 bar and button fastenings became fashionable and shoes became more pointed with high waisted heels. As many as three bars reached high on the instep. As the fashion for bar and button shoes remained for so long, the height and shape of heels and the blunt or pointed toes were the main variations, although those with high insteps tended to have a T-shaped bar. Large bows or buckles were also popular as they could hide the elastic beneath to give the shoe a better fit. Quite often toecaps and the back of the shoes were decorated in a punched-out design.

Court shoes (first worn at Court) became very fashionable in the early 1900s. These were plain shoes with heels of any height, the toe shapes following prevailing fashions. These shoes were worn on formal occasions and for evening wear when they were made of satins or brocades as well as soft leather. In the 1920s sling-back court shoes became fashionable.

Ankle boots with cloth tops, buttoned to simulate spats were popular from the late 1800s. High, cloth boots became fashionable when skirts became shorter, and they were made to look like court shoes with gaiters. Some boots were ornately decorated with coloured stitching with toecaps in different colours; they were scalloped on the buttonhole sides, and the tops were fur-trimmed. When motoring first became commonplace, cars were unheated and this brought about a new fashion for foot muffs and overshoes lined in a warm material.

Stockings were still of ribbed silk, lisle or wool and decorated with clocks or lace insertions until about 1912 when artificial silk was introduced. About 1913 pale colours became fashionable for evening wear and although black remained the most popular for day wear, greens and

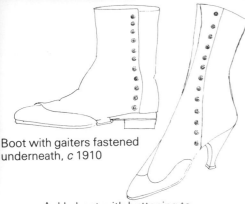

Boot with gaiters fastened underneath, c 1910

Ankle boot with buttoning to simulate gaiters. The toe cap is in a contrasting colour, c 1918

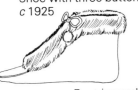

Shoe with three button fastening, c 1925

Fur trimmed boot, c 1925

Various shoes (a) c 1901. (b) c 1920. (c) c 1919. (d) c 1924. (e) c 1925. (f) c 1918

purples were also seen until the 1920s when lighter colours such as beige, grey or pink were also worn.

Headwear

Bonnets were being replaced by *hats* or *toques*. Until about 1905 the brims were wide and turned up, the back ornamented with trimmings and flowers. Tricorne shaped hats were also popular at the start of the century. Veils were mainly black, either plain or with spots.

From about 1907 hats had full crowns with large drooping brims. *Trilby* shaped hats gradually replaced the smaller straw boaters and sailor hats for sports and these were also worn with tailor-mades. Hats for motoring, although large, were held down with hatpins and veils. The large hats of the Edwardian era were often held in place with long hatpins whose heads were ornamented with jewels or carved ivory designs.

About 1911 tall-crowned hats became more fashionable than those with the very wide brims and were trimmed with ribbons or tulle and feathers.

When the crowns of hats again became lower in 1912 the feather decorations stood upright and the hats were worn tilted forward, but during the First World War high-crowned toques and wide-brimmed hats similar to those of the Edwardian times, became fashionable again and remained so until the early 1920s.

Hats worn in the summer were made of straw or in tulle, the large hats being profusely decorated or draped with chiffon. For winter, felt was used extensively and the hats were plainer with less decoration.

In the early 1920s hats were made of softer velours or cloth and the brims were often pulled down on the head. The close fitting crowns gave a cloche appearance. Trimmings were closer to the hats and sometimes appliquéd designs or bows were attached; ribbon hatbands with buckles were also seen.

Berets, sometimes knitted, were first really popular in the 1920s.

For evening wear bandeaux as well as sequined turbans adorned with feathers and plumes were very popular until the 1930s, after which feathers and flowers or sequined veils alone were worn.

Hairstyles

The hairstyles of the 1890s were still the fashion in the first decade of the twentieth century. Hair was still dressed high in front over pads with the back swept up. This could be in a coil or plait. Soft puffs or waves were very fashionable and to give more fullness to the hair, apart from adding false pieces, it was backcombed. Marcel waving was still much in use, as permanent waving, introduced in 1904, took too long and was still very expensive. Hair was held in place with hairpins and combs, and for evening wear these were decorated with flowers, feathers and jewels. By about 1908 hairstyles were given emphasis towards the back of the head with large twisted buns or loose curls held in place with ribbons. The sides were puffed out even more, especially when the large hats became fashionable. Centre partings were often seen with the hair in full soft waves either side.

In the second decade the hair at the top of the head was not so high and

Headwear (a) *c* 1901. (b) *c* 1906

Various headwear, 1924-25

Deep crowned cloche hat. The hair
is worn in an 'earphone' style,
c 1924

Decorated turban style hat, *c* 1929

Eton crop
style, *c* 1924

Short hair with a fringe, *c* 1924

Hairpiece with a loop at the top,
c 1925

Various hairstyles (a) *c* 1907.
(b) *c* 1910. (c) *c* 1910. (d) *c* 1915.
(e) *c* 1920. (f) *c* 1924

67

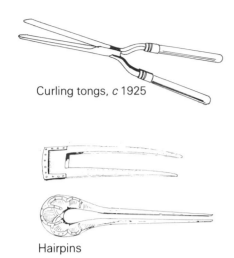

Curling tongs, c 1925

Hairpins

Decorated neckband

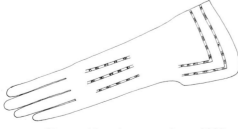

Soft leather handbag, c 1920

Glove with a short gauntlet, c 1929

the sides were less wide, the mass being concentrated between the nape and the crown, in a Grecian style. Although hairstyles were still quite elaborate at the beginning of the First World War, it was impractical to have bouffant hairstyles whilst doing war work, especially in factories, so hair became shorter and was worn closer to the head in a bun or coil at the back. By the end of the war very short hairstyles became the mode. These were known as bobs, the hair cut straight across the forehead. Hair was usually parted to one side, more usually on the left, held on the other side with a slide or comb. Coiled plaits worn around the ears, as earphones, or tight curls rolled under, were other means to give a short hair appearance. By the 1920s looser and more windswept styles appeared and by 1923 it was fashionable to wear wide bands around the head over the forehead. These bands were often embroidered and for evening wear were also encrusted with jewels.

About 1925 a more sophisticated hairstyle known as the *Eton crop* became the mode. It was cut straight above ear level, the sides left longer to curl forward to the cheeks. For evening weart a postiche was often added to give a longer and softer appearance. By the end of the 1920s and beginning of the 1930s hairstyles again became longer and softer with waves and small clusters of curls.

Beauty aids and accessories

In the Edwardian era until about 1920 women had tried to make themselves look mature. In the early 1890s make-up was still crudely made, but when it became more popular, cosmetics were developed professionally.

Vivid lip colour was first fashionable in the 1920s and was the most popular form of make-up, although eye shadow was already being used in the early 1890s having been popularised by Diaghlev's Russian Ballet. Rouge on the cheeks was applied over a chalky white powder as palour was still fashionable until the 1930s when sunburnt complexions became the mode.

Advances in chemistry allowed lipsticks and rouge to be made in a greater range of reds which blended with coloured face powders.

In the 1920s lips were shaped into Cupid's bows and plucked eyebrows were pencilled in to the required shape. Eyelids were also coloured in blues for evenings, whilst they were made shiny with lanolin for daywear.

Mascara was first made in blocks, moistened and applied with a special brush to darken eyelashes.

Handkerchiefs, so popular previously, were just carried in handbags as a necessity, except when worn in a top pocket of a tailormade jacket. Lace handkerchiefs were still decorative for evening wear in the early 1900s.

Gloves were usually made of leather or wool, fur also being popular in the winter, and gave a better fit when they were buttoned at the wrists, sometimes into the palms. By the 1920s elastic insets at the wrist became more practical. Gauntlet gloves also remained in fashion.

For evening wear gloves were made of softer leathers or silk and were long to the elbows, fastened with up to twenty buttons, being left open at the wrist so that they could be taken off the hands and allowed to hang loosely. They were often decorated with beads and embroidery.

In really cold weather overgloves or mittens with a thumb piece and bag

Hobble fetters, *c* 1911

Muff, *c* 1904

Leather handbag with a metal frame and clasp, *c* 1926

Ornamental buckle

Silk sunshade, *c* 1902

for the remaining fingers were often worn over more elegant lightweight gloves. Mitts that were in fact fingerless gloves were worn on formal occasions, made of black or white lace.

Muffs in various shapes and sizes remained fashionable into the 1920s, chain or ribbons being attached so that they could hang around the neck leaving the hands free.

Feather *boas* and tasselled scarves were popular at the start of the century when they could reach the ground, but by about 1909 they became knee length. For evening wear long, fringed shawls were also popular. About 1921 *stoles* and shoulder capes were made of fox tails with a fox's head centre back, the front fastening with hooks and eyes concealed by paws.

Scarves, mainly of silk or chiffon, were very popular worn in a variety of ways. They could be draped loosely to one side over the shoulders or worn knotted at the base of V shaped décolletages. From about 1924 handpainted designs were not unusual. Collars and cuffs usually of white linen were made detachable for easier cleaning as well as interchanging.

Handbags were at first rather small. They could be envelope shaped with several compartments inside. As bags became larger they were made in various shapes and on a metal frame with a snap closure and matching leather handles so that they could be suspended from the arm. By 1929 it became fashionable for handbags to be made to match shoes.

For evening wear *Dorothy bags*, closed with a drawstring at the top, were made of brocades or beadwork. Bags in other shapes were also made in these fabrics as well as petit point embroidery. Gold or silver metal chainwork was also very fashionable.

Before the First World War feather *fans* were fashionable again for evening wear. Lace or other materials with painted designs as well as beads and sequins could be seen on folding fans.

Until the 1930s *parasols* were carried mainly as decoration or used against the sun. They were often lined and edged with lace or fringing. The handles were usually long and delicate with ornate knobs of china or metal. *Unbrellas*, used in rainy weather, had larger shades than parasols and were generally of black silk. Collapsable or telescopic handles with sliding and extending ribs were first seen in the mid 1920s.

Diamonds and pearls the two favourite stones use in *jewellery*, and silver was one of the most popular of metals. Enamelled designs were seen on brooches. A great deal of artificial jewellery was also worn. Long, pendant earrings became fashionable in the 1920s and could be made to screw on to the ears as well as being made for pierced ears. Rings with diamond clusters and perhaps a coloured stone or pearl in the centre could be made in oblong shapes. Brooches were worn on the shoulder or corsage and were mainly rectangular from the 1920s. Anklets or ankle bracelets were fashionable in the 1920s. Bead or pearl necklaces, long or short were mainly worn with tailor-made suits.

Metal hooks and eyes, bars or loops of thread were a popular method of fastening, as well as buttons; press studs were first seen about 1905.

Zip fasteners were first manufactured in England in 1919 and came into general use in the mid 1920s as fastenings on dresses and skirts, usually on the left side or at the back.

Glossary of Terms

Barbe   Long, pleated piece of linen worn under the chin.

Barbette   Similar to a wimple.

Basque   Short skirt added to a bodice at the waist.

Bertha   Silk or lace frills covering shoulders and a low décolletage.

Bicorne   Hat with brim turned up front and back.

Bishop sleeve   Full from the shoulders to wrist, where it was gathered to a band.

Boa   Long stole or scarf.

Bolero   Short loose fitting jacket, the fronts curving away, usually sleeveless.

Bombast   Horsehair or wool padding.

Buffon   Fine material puffed up, covering a décolletage.

Bum roll   Padded roll worn to widen the hips.

Buskin   Boots, reaching the knees.

Bustle   Half cage of whalebone or other stiffener to support the fullness of a skirt behind.

Caul   As Crespine. Headcovering in gold or silver net with jewels similar to a fret.

Calash   High hood folded on hoops, worn with a tall headdress.

Chaperon   Hood with a liripipe.

Chatelaine   Ornamental chain from which were hung various items.

Chemise   Undergarment of a soft material.

Chopine   Wooden overshoes, built high with cork or wooden soles.

Chignon   Mass of hair arranged in a loop or ringlets hanging behind.

Chiton   Rectangular piece of material sewn up the sides and fastened with a fibula at the shoulders.

Cloche hat   Bell shaped, close fitting, worn well down.

Clocks   Embroidered decoration on the outside edge of stockings.

Coif   Close fitting cap, sometimes worn as an undercap.

Commode   Wire frame to support the lace tiers of a fontange headdress.

Corsage   Upper or bodice part of dress.

Corset   Undergarment reinforced with whalebone stays.

Cote-hardie   Close fitting overgarment fastening down the front.

Covert coat   Short, fly-fronted overcoat.

Crêve-coeur   Curls at the nape of the neck.

Crespine   Similar to a caul, shaped like a bag with jewels at the intersections.

Doublet   Close fitting waisted jacket.

Echelles   Ribbon bow trimmings down a stomacher.

En tablier   Decorated and pleated front, like an apron.

Farthingale   Hoops usually of whalebone or wire to distend shirts.

Fichu   Softly draped collar.

Fillet   Narrow band worn around the head, or a stiffened linen band worn with a barbette.

Fitchet   Vertical placket pocket in a side seam.

Fontange headdress   Small flat linen cap with lace tiers and pendants behind.

Flounce   Deep frill gathered or pleated, as decoration.

Fourreau   Skirt and bodice cut in one.

French hood   Small bonnet-type hood made on a stiffened frame.

Fret   Skull cap or coif in a trellis work design.

Frontlet   Decorative loop suspended over the forehead, worn with head attire.

Gable headdress   Similar to an English hood, the front shaped like a gable.

Gaiters   Ankle coverings spreading over the top of footwear and fastened with a strap beneath.

Garters   Narrow bands tied above or below the knees to hold up stockings.

Gigot sleeves   Full at the shoulder and becoming tight at the wrists, the top sometimes distended by hoops.

Goffers   Flutes or ruffles in small pleats made with a goffering iron.

Gore   Triangular peice of material, narrow at the top to give flaring.

Gorget   Cape part of a hood or chaperon.

Habit shirt   Fill-in for a day dress, sometimes with a small neck ruff.

Headraile   Square kerchief folded diagonally and worn towards the back of the head.

Hennin   Steeple-shaped headdress.

Hobble skirt   Narrow, tapering to the ankles, sometimes with a side slit.

Hoops   Whalebone or cane circles sewn into an under petticoat to distend skirts.

Houppelande   Voluminous upper gown falling in tubular folds, often with wide sleeves.

Imbecile sleeves   Full sleeves gathered at the wrist with a cuff.

Jabot   Lace cravat or frill.

Jet   Black polished mineral used in jewellery and for buttons.

Kirtle   Undergarment worn like a petticoat.

Knickerbockers   Loose breeches to the knees and gathered to a band.

Lappet   Pendants hanging from either side or back of a headdress.

Lettice cap   Triangular shaped bonnet, rising to a crown and covering the ears.

Liripipe   Long pendant of a chaperon or hood.

Louis heel   The sole continuing up the arch and down the front of the heel.

Mancherons   Very short oversleeves.

Medici collar   Net or lace standing up round the back, sloping down in front.

Mittens   Gloves with a thumb and another section for the fingers.

Mitts   Fingerless gloves.

Negligée   Informal attire.

Open robe   Open from waist to reveal a decorated petticoat.

Palisade   Wire frame to support a high headdress or hairstyle.

Palla   Rectangular outer garment, sometimes open one side.

Panes   Parallel slashings or narrow strips of material joined at the ends to give the impression of slashings.

Pannier   Skirt drapery, bunched at the hips.

Pantaloons   Straight long-legged drawers.

Partlet   Decorated cover for a low décolletage, similar to a sleeveless jacket, underbodice or kerchief.

Pattens   Overshoes, usually of wood, secured by leather straps.

Pelisse robe   Day dress fastened down the front.

Peplos   Loose gown worn over a chiton.

Peplum   Short overskirt, slightly longer behind, attached to the waist.

Pet-en-l'air   Long jacket with a sac back.

Peter Pan collar   flat, attached to a rounded neckline and ending with rounded ends.

Petticoat   Underskirt that could be decorated.

Pinner   (a) Hanging streamers on headwear. (b) Fill-in for a low décolletage.

Plastron   Front panel of skirt or bodice, usually in a